EMPIRES OF
THE MAYA

GREAT EMPIRES OF THE PAST

Empire of Alexander the Great

Empire of Ancient Egypt

Empire of Ancient Greece

Empire of Ancient Rome

Empire of the Aztecs

Empire of the Incas

Empire of the Islamic World

Empire of the Mongols

Empires of Ancient Mesopotamia

Empires of Ancient Persia

Empires of Medieval West Africa

Empires of the Maya

GREAT EMPIRES OF THE PAST

EMPIRES OF THE MAYA

JILL RUBALCABA

ANGELA KELLER, HISTORICAL CONSULTANT

CHELSEA HOUSE
PUBLISHERS
An imprint of Infobase Publishing

Great Empires of the Past: Empires of the Maya

Chelsea House
An imprint of Infobase Publishing
132 West 31st Street
New York NY 10001

Library of Congress Cataloging-in-Publication Data
Rubalcaba, Jill.
  Empires of the Maya / Jill Rubalcaba.
      p. cm.—(Great empires of the past)
  Includes bibliographical references and index.
  ISBN 978-1-60413-155-0
  1. Mayas—History—Juvenile literature. 2. Mayas—Social life and customs—Juvenile literature. I. Title. II. Series.

  F1435.R83 2009
  972.8101—dc22   2009021502

Chelsea House books are available at special discounts when purchased in bulk quantities for businesses, associations, institutions, or sales promotions. Please call our Special Sales Department in New York at (212) 967-8800 or (800) 322-8755.

You can find Chelsea House on the World Wide Web at http://www.chelseahouse.com

Produced by the Shoreline Publishing Group LLC
Editorial Director: James Buckley Jr.
Series Editor: Beth Adelman
Text design by Annie O'Donnell
Cover design by Alicia Post
Composition by Mary Susan Ryan-Flynn
Cover printed by Bang Printing, Brainerd, MN
Book printed and bound by Bang Printing, Brainerd, MN
Date printed: December 2009

Printed in the United States of America

10 9 8 7 6 5 4 3 2 1

This book is printed on acid-free paper.

All links and Web addresses were checked and verified to be correct at the time of publication. Because of the dynamic nature of the Web, some addresses and links may have changed since publication and may no longer be valid.

CONTENTS

INTRODUCTION

VOLCANO PEAKS PIERCE THE BLANKET OF COOL MIST that hangs above the forest canopy. Ghostly howler monkeys scream, unseen, as if the ruined temples were part of a scene in an unearthly horror movie. For some, the sounds create the illusion that the lost city of Copán is haunted by tortured souls wailing deep within the stone pyramids. Only the occasional rustle of a tree branch reveals that the monkeys are the true source of the screams. They scramble across a platform where priests once addressed thousands of people. The platform is now buried in vines, and moss, and jungle growth.

The remains of Copán, one of the richest centers of Maya civilization, lie deep in the tropical forest of modern Honduras. Copán became wealthy because of its rich soil and the Copán River's annual flood. Each year, the river overflowed and the water left behind a new layer of rich, fertile soil. The huge quantity of precious jade found in the tombs of Copán's kings is evidence of how wealthy they were.

MAYA GEOGRAPHY

The land of the ancient Maya lies south of the Tropic of Cancer and north of the Equator in what is now called the Yucatán Peninsula, Guatemala, Belize, southern Mexico, and western Honduras and El Salvador. There are a number of different habitats within the Maya area, but for convenience, scholars divide it into three major geographic zones: the Pacific coastal plain in the south, the highlands in the middle, and the lowlands in the north.

OPPOSITE
The Maya were master pyramid builders, but their magnificent cities were buried by the jungle until the late 1800s and early 1900s. This is a pyramid in Chichén Itzá, a great Maya city of the Postclassic Era.

CONNECTIONS

What Are Connections?

Throughout this book, and all the books in the Great Empires of the Past series, there are Connections boxes. They point out ideas, inventions, art, food, customs, and more from this empire that are still part of the world today. Nations and cultures in remote history can seem far away from the present day, but these connections demonstrate how our everyday lives have been shaped by the peoples of the past.

The earliest Maya settlements rose alongside the areas that are now mangrove swamps near the Pacific coast. This food-rich environment was ideal for supporting year-round living. There was sea life on the coast and rich farmland not far inland. The coastal plain became a prime location for growing cacao, which is used to make chocolate. The Maya from the coastal plain traded cacao throughout the entire Maya area. Even today, large agricultural businesses dominate the plain. The main crops now are sugarcane, cotton, and cattle.

The highlands are mountainous. This region is the most diverse of the three zones. The southern half of the highlands is volcanically active, and the rich, deep soils developed out of ancient lava flows and ash deposits from the nearby volcanoes. For thousands of years, large numbers of people chose to live here despite the dangers of earthquakes and volcanic eruptions. It was worth the risk because the volcanic ash made the soil excellent for growing plants.

Fewer people lived in the mountains in the northern half of the highlands. Here the ancient Maya mined obsidian (volcanic glass), jade, and other semi-precious stones. The rainforest of the northern highlands sprawls down into lower elevations and tropical climates.

The gentle hills of the southern lowlands, called the Petén region, are covered with forest and laced with rivers. The Petén gently blends into the dry bushland of the northern lowlands, or the Yucatán Peninsula, where water resources are limited and are found mostly below ground.

CLASSIFYING MAYA HISTORY

Archaeologists divide pre-Columbian (the time before Columbus arrived in the Americas in 1492 C.E.) Maya history into three major time periods: Preclassic, Classic, and Postclassic. During the Preclassic Era, from about 1200 B.C.E. to 250 C.E., settled farming communities grew into complex societies. Many Maya kingdoms experienced rapid growth in this era. They built monumental structures, established long-distance trade routes, and developed governing systems. In the later part of the Preclassic Era, some kingdoms were enjoying their peak while others had already faded away.

The Classic Era was between about 250 and 900. From southeastern Mexico to upper Central America, this varied landscape supported millions of people in Classic times. During the height of Maya civilization in the eighth century, as many as 60 independent kingdoms dotted the Maya area, as well as hundreds of smaller towns and villages.

Unlike the Aztec people, their neighbors to the north, the Maya never unified into a single empire. Instead, they built commerce centers that grew into city-states (cities that function as separate kingdoms or

IN THEIR OWN WORDS

Peeling Back the Jungle

By the time the Spanish conquered Honduras in the 1520s, Copán had long been overgrown by rainforest. Several explorers visited it in the early 19th century and wrote about the barely visible ruins. In 1839, explorer and travel writer John Lloyd Stephens (1805–1852) paid a Maya guide to lead him to the site. In Stephens's book *Incidents of Travel in Central America, Chiapas and Yucatan,* he offers this riveting account of how the jungle was stripped away to rediscover the ruins.

> It is impossible to describe the interest with which I explored these ruins. The ground was entirely new; there were no guide-books or guides; the whole was virgin soil. We could not see 10 yards before us, and never knew what we should stumble upon next. At one time we stopped to cut away branches and vines which concealed the face of a monument, and then to dig around and bring to light a fragment, a sculptured corner of which protruded from the earth. I leaned over with breathless anxiety while the Indians worked, and an eye, an ear, a foot, or a hand was disentombed. When the machete rang against the chiseled stone, I pushed the Indians away, and cleared out the loose earth with my hands. The beauty of the sculpture, the solemn stillness of the woods, disturbed only by the scrambling of monkeys and chattering of parrots, the desolation of the city, and the mystery that hung over it, all created an interest higher, if possible, than I had ever felt among the ruins of the Old World.

(Source: Stephens, John Lloyd. *Incidents of Travel*. Available online. "Lost King of the Maya." URL: http://www.pbs.org/wgbh/nova/maya/travel.html. Accessed September 23, 2008.)

Palenque was one of the great cities of the Classic Era. These ruins were once the temple complex.

nations) ruled by kings. These kingdoms formed alliances with one another one day, only to turn into sworn enemies the next.

Robert J. Sharer wrote in *The Ancient Maya* that the capitals of independent kingdoms were "interconnected by commerce, alliances, and rivalries that often led to war." By the end of the Classic Era, the southern lowland capitals had collapsed, leaving modern scholars to wonder what catastrophe forced the Maya to abandon their cities.

The northern lowlands kingdoms rose and fell during the Postclassic Era, from 900 to 1524. Some kingdoms flowered dramatically, but probably did not reach the heights of the kingdoms from previous eras. It was in the Postclassic Era that kings lost their grip on centralized power and nobles greedily stepped in to break the kingdoms up into smaller pieces.

The Postclassic Era ended with the arrival of the Spaniards, who found that most Maya were living in medium-sized kingdoms and groups of allied cities throughout the Maya area.

HOW HISTORIANS KNOW ABOUT THE MAYA

What is known about the Maya comes from many sources. Scholars piece together bits of information as one would put together a jigsaw puzzle—each piece contributing to the whole picture. Archaeologists unearth buildings or just their foundations, and map Maya cities. They dig up royal tombs and speculate about the lives of the living by examining what was buried with them when they died. Geologists date towns by counting carbon atoms in the garbage the Maya threw away. Biologists reconstruct Maya diets by examining teeth and bones.

Scientists from every field contribute a piece to the puzzle—linguists, historians, anthropologists (people who study human cultures), mathematicians, ecologists, geneticists. Even NASA's scientists are adding a piece to the puzzle by locating stone structures using satellites that circle the Earth.

Much information comes from the Maya themselves. Hieroglyphs (writing using symbols) cover Maya stone and wooden monuments, doorjambs, wall panels, benches, and stairways like graffiti. It was not until the mid-20th century that Mayanists (people who study the Maya) realized this was a writing system that had elements such as those in modern writing systems, where symbols can indicate sounds. And it was decades more before the 800 signs in the Maya writing system were decoded. Today, Mayanists are scrambling to translate public carvings and paintings that commemorate important moments, date kings and kingdoms, and chronicle the lives of kings and their courts.

These public billboards reveal details of the people in power, but what about the common people? What kind of life did the farmer lead? What about mothers and children, artists and builders? For details about everyday life and everyday people, scholars carefully study smaller archaeological sites and households. They also look at accounts written by the Spaniards who came to the Maya area in the 16th century.

One particularly detailed account was written by a Franciscan priest who arrived in the Yucatán in 1544. Diego de Landa (1524–1579) had been sent to bring the Catholic religion to the native peoples. But he became obsessed with wiping out Maya customs and rituals. Landa claimed Maya books taught pagan beliefs (that is, non-Christian beliefs that he considered primitive) and he destroyed every Maya book he found. In July of 1562, Landa burned more than 5,000 Maya images and dozens of Maya books that he believed to be works of the devil. Books written by the Maya about medicine, astronomy, religion, and history were all burned.

Maya or Mayan?

There are some conventions among scholars about when to use *Maya* and when to use *Mayan*. *Maya* can be used as a noun when speaking about the Maya people then and now. *Maya* can also be used as an adjective to describe something that is part of the Maya culture, such as Maya monuments or Maya pottery. Scholars use the word *Mayan* to refer to the language of the Maya, as in, "The Mayan word for turtle is *ahk.*"

CONNECTIONS

Rainman

Shamans—people who had access to and influence over good and evil spirits—were an essential part of Maya society. They still play an important role today. A village shaman could be called upon to cure disease, make crops grow, or conduct religious ceremonies. Today's shamans offer prayers to ancient gods and goddesses. They preserve a link to the past and to the Maya people's unique view of the world.

In 1989, during a terrible drought in the Yucatán, the people called on a shaman to bring rain. A shaman named Don Pablo conducted a three-day ceremony to the storm gods called the Cha-Chac ceremony.

Maya archaeologist David Friedel described the shaman and the rain he brought in *The Untold Story of the Ancient Maya:* "Don Pablo came running over the crest of a nearby hill, clutching his hat in the gusting winds as he fled inches ahead of a gray wall of rain. A great rainbow arched over him in brilliant orange light of the setting sun in a magnificent display that affirmed the success of his performance as shaman."

The Spanish king condemned Landa's actions and commanded him to come back to Spain to stand trial for abusing his power. During Landa's trial, as part of his defense, he wrote a book describing his observations of the Maya people, their culture, and their writing system. One version of this book is *Relacion de las Cosas de Yucatan* (an account of the affairs of Yucatán), which was later translated into English using the title *Yucatan Before and After the Conquest.*

Landa was found innocent and returned to the Yucatán in 1573 as bishop of the region. His book provides an important glimpse into the Maya way of life at the end of pre-Columbian times. Although Landa was responsible for erasing the Maya's own historical account, he is also responsible for much of what is known about the Maya today. His information was based on his own observations and extensive interviews with the Maya people he met. Still, it is important to remember that the book was written by someone who respected what the Maya had achieved but was angered by their religious beliefs.

Very few Maya books survived Landa's fires. Even fewer survived the passage of time. After Landa's great book burning, there were also some attempts to write down from memory—or possibly copy from books that were hidden—the classic Maya texts. One such text is the *Chilam Balam. Chilam* is the Mayan word for priest or shaman, and *balam* means jaguar, which is a prestigious title. The Maya called their powerful priests *chilam balam,* or jaguar priests. There are several *Chilam Balam* books from various cities in Yucatán. The most famous are the *Chilam Balam of Chumayel* and the *Chilam Balam of Tizimin.*

The Books that Survived the Fire

Diego de Landa wrote in *Yucatan Before and After the Conquest,* "We found a large number of books. . . and as they contained nothing in which there were not to be seen superstition and lies of the devil, we burned them all, which they regretted to an amazing degree, and which caused them much affliction."

The texts that did survive the fires were all documents from the Postclassic Era. They were written in Mayan hieroglyphs. All were sent back to Europe, where no one knew how to read them, and they were kept as curiosities.

Today, these ancient books are known as *codices* (books made from bark and written in hieroglyphic script; the singular is *codex*). Only three Maya codices and fragments of a fourth survived the book-burning. They are named after the cities in Europe where they are now located. They are:

Dresden Codex: This beautifully illustrated codex was made by flattening a long sheet of bark into paper and then whitening the surface with lime paste. The book was constructed by folding the long sheet accordion style to create 74 pages. It contains almanacs, mathematical tables for eclipses, predictions about floods and when to plant, as well as information about sickness and cures.

Madrid Codex: Some scholars believe that the Madrid Codex is a table for eclipses.

(continues)

A beautiful page from the Dresden Codex has tables showing the phases of Venus alongside pictures of Maya gods.

(continued)

Eclipse symbols appear on many of the pages. Celestial serpents snake across pages 12 through 18. The Maya often used serpents as symbols for the sky. The Mayan word *chan* means both "sky" and "snake." Also included in the Madrid Codex are tips on deer hunting, deer trapping, beekeeping, marriage, and how to summon the rain.

Paris Codex: This codex illustrates 13 constellations, each represented by mystical animals carrying the sun glyph (symbol) in their mouth. The arrangement of the constellations is similar to modern signs of the zodiac. The information in the Paris Codex guided priests in their divinations by revealing to them the workings of the universe.

Grolier Codex: Small pieces are all that is left of this badly damaged codex, found by treasure hunters in a cave in Chiapas, Mexico. The codex fragments are bits of a Venus table, predicting with precision when the planet Venus will appear as the morning star. The *Manuscript of Serna*, a missionary report from Central Mexico (as quoted in "The Real Maya Prophecies: Astronomy in the Inscriptions and Codices"), states that next to the sun, the natives "adored and made more sacrifices" to Venus than any other "celestial or terrestrial creatures."

Although the text of these versions of *Chilam Balam* was written in the Maya language, the script is European. The supposed author, Chilam Balam, was said to have been a great Maya priest from the 15th century. But in fact, the *Chilam Balam* books were written by several people over several generations. They record centuries of history before, during, and after the Spanish conquest of the Maya area.

Many towns had their own version of *Chilam Balam*. Although it was written down, the people knew *Chilam Balam* through firelight performances. These were chanted by the priests who protected the book, and accompanied by moans of conch-shell trumpets, clickety-clacks of bone rattles, and the mellow thump of wooden and clay drums. The messages chanted were often mysterious, with animals and plants serving as symbols for something else entirely. For example, jaguars and eagles stood for the most important leaders, foxes represented the Spanish invaders, and deer symbolized the Maya people.

The Maya took the prophecies in *Chilam Balam* very seriously. They believed that the gods had revealed to the jaguar priests what would happen in the future, and it was the job of the *chilam* to relay that information to them. One important role of a Maya shaman was to be a diviner—someone who interpreted the ancient texts and sacred calendars. To the Maya, history was circular and repeated at regular intervals. So by carefully studying the past, one could predict the future.

Another piece of the Maya puzzle is provided by understanding their mythology. In the 16th century, the Quiche Maya living in the highlands of present-day Guatemala wrote down the *Popol Vuh* (council book). *Popol Vuh* is considered one of the greatest works of Native American literature, in part because it is one of the very few records of early mythology in all of the Americas.

The first half of *Popol Vuh* is a poem more than 9,000 lines long. The poem is a retelling of Maya creation myths that go back to the very origins of the Maya themselves. The creation myths show how the Maya viewed their universe. The second half of *Popol Vuh* is the history of the Quiche kingdom—their kings and the connection between humans and gods.

IN THEIR OWN WORDS

Bad Times to Come

This prophecy (prediction of the future) from the book of *Chilam Balam of Chumayel* predicts a severe drought. It says water will become so scarce that watering holes will dry up and deer will die. During a long drought, the Maya would leave their villages and wander through the forests looking for people who would take their possessions in exchange for food. This passage predicts a future drought so devastating even the ruler will be forced to beg for food and will be unable to provide for himself or his people. (A *k'atun* is a cycle of time in the Maya calendar.)

Submit to the unhappy destiny of the katun which is to come. If you do not submit, you shall be moved from where your feet are rooted. If you do not submit, you shall gnaw the trunks of trees and herbs. If you do not submit, it shall be as when the deer die, so that they go forth from your settlement. Then [even] when the ruler [himself] goes forth, he shall return within your settlement bearing nothing. Also there shall come [such a pestilence that] the vultures enter the houses, a time of great death among the wild animals. . . .

(Source: Roys, Ralph L., translator. *The Book of Chilam Balam of Chumayel*. Washington, D.C.: Carnegie Institution, 1933.)

THE MAYA LEGACY

The Maya left behind thousands of grand stone monuments and structures—temples, palaces, and pyramids inscribed (painted or engraved) with scenes from Maya mythology and portraits of powerful kings. Over a 2,000-year span, these kings ruled over nobles, priests, merchants, artisans, warriors, farmers, and slaves. Maya kings financed ambitious construction projects such as buildings, reservoirs, and causeways (raised roadways). They paid for these things with wealth gained through conquests, tribute (wealth given to a ruler to show submission), and a trade network that reached far beyond the Maya world into Central America and Central Mexico.

Although the individual kingdoms never united into one grand empire, all Maya people were united by their spiritual view of the universe, their mythology, their calendar, and their culture. What divided them ended up saving them—at least for a while. Spanish military leaders and their armies of conquistadors were able to conquer the Aztec people and topple their empire merely by taking Tenochtitlán, the Aztec capital city. The conquest of the Maya would take centuries. It required waging war a hundred times over, in hundreds of settlements throughout the Maya area.

Many scholars consider the Maya culture to be the most complex of any ancient Western Hemisphere culture. Sharer wrote in *The Ancient Maya,* "The more we learn about the Maya past, the more profound is our respect. For as the record shows, the Maya were a people of astonishing achievement in mathematics, astronomy, calendar-making, and writing; in technology, political organization, and commerce; in sculpture, painting, architecture, and the other arts."

PART · 1

HISTORY

THE PRECLASSIC ERA:
DAWN OF THE MAYA

THE CLASSIC ERA:
RISE AND FALL OF THE SUPERPOWERS

THE POSTCLASSIC ERA:
RISE OF THE YUCATÁN

CHAPTER 1

THE PRECLASSIC ERA: DAWN OF THE MAYA

THE PRESENT WORLD BEGAN AUGUST 11, 3114 B.C.E., according to the ancient Maya calendar known as the Long Count. The Long Count kept track of how many days, or *kins,* passed since that very first day. The Maya calendar counted 360 *kins* in a year. Each year was called a *tun,* the Mayan word for "stone." The ancient Maya were the only pre-Columbian people to keep a calendar with a specific starting point.

What was the Maya world like at the time of their "creation" more than 5,000 years ago? Scholars call this time the Archaic Era (*archaic* means very old). This is when ancient peoples in the Americas were making the change from hunting and gathering wild plants to settled village life and agriculture.

The change was gradual. It spanned thousands of years, from 6000 to 2000 B.C.E. The shift began as Archaic peoples started returning to the same spots each season. Perhaps fish ran at a certain time of year in a particular stream. Or nuts ripened in a favorite grove. The people returned year after year until they were no longer wandering about randomly, looking for food, but were beginning a settled life.

Scholars do not know exactly when Archaic peoples first started farming in Mesoamerica (the area extending from what is today central Mexico to Honduras and Nicaragua). But they do know that there is a connection between agriculture and settled life. And they know that by about 1000 B.C.E, farming and the settled life that goes with it were widely adopted in Mesoamerica.

In the beginning, Archaic peoples did not practice farming the way it is done now. Instead, they simply encouraged certain plants to grow at their favorite spots by weeding and watering. When it came

OPPOSITE

Beautifully carved stelae throughout the ancient Maya world use glyphs to trace Maya history and proclaim the accomplishments of kings.

to harvesting, they picked the best plants—the heartiest growers with the most seeds. By selecting these choice plants, they slowly changed the wild plants into plants that were especially suited to farming.

These early farmers began adapting their tools, and developing new ones, to prepare their foods. Two tools that were adapted for farming were the *mano* and *metate*. These stones were originally used for grinding seeds, but later became important for grinding corn. They were made from basalt (black rock formed from hardened lava) or granite. Women ground grains on a basalt slab (called *metate*) using a rock shaped like a rolling pin with flattened sides (the *mano*).

Archaic peoples 5,000 years ago also collected raw materials from distant places. These materials included obsidian, which is a volcanic glass that can be flaked (shaped by banging with a fist-sized rock called a *cobble*) into razor-sharp blades. They collected jade, chocolate, feathers, and other goods and traded with other groups of people for obsidian and volcanic rocks such as basalt. As the complexity of these Maya ancestors' lives increased, they moved toward settled life and the beginning of a new era.

THE OLMECS

Before the Maya culture emerged in the Preclassic Era, a civilization sometimes called the "mother civilization" arose in Mesoamerica from about 2000 to 1000 B.C.E. The people who created this civilization lived in the swampy south coast of what is today the Gulf of Mexico. Although historians do not know what the people called themselves, modern scholars call them the Olmecs. The Olmecs were the first Mesoamericans to establish communities led by a chief, or chiefdoms.

Three of the most important Olmec centers were La Venta, San Lorenzo, and Laguna de los Cerros. Each of the three centers controlled a different vital resource. In the east, La Venta dominated the fertile coastal plain where the Olmecs

CONNECTIONS

The *Mano* and *Metate*

The stone grinding tools used by the Maya, *mano* and *metate*, can still be found in Mesoamerican markets today. The substance to be ground—perhaps corn or cacao beans—is spread out on the flat *metate*. A flattened side of the *mano* is then pushed over the grains, crushing them. Today's Mesoamericans believe there is no better tool for grinding corn for tortillas and mixing cacao for chocolate.

The Olmecs are famous for their giant carvings of heads. These huge stones weigh an average of 20 tons.

grew maize (corn), cacao (the plant from which chocolate is made), and rubber, and extracted salt from ocean waters.

At the center of the Olmec area was San Lorenzo, the oldest Olmec settlement. This center controlled trade routes. Laguna de los Cerros was at the foot of volcanic mountains where basalt was quarried (dug out) and used for monuments and *metates*.

The Olmecs are most famous for carving giant round basalt rocks into heads of rulers. One head is estimated to weigh 40 tons. Stones for these monuments were quarried as far as 80 miles away. Gangs of thousands of men dragged stones weighing an average of 20 tons back to their settlements. They most likely used huge log rafts to travel over water and log rollers to travel over land.

The Olmecs also carved stelae (upright stone slabs with carvings on them) and altars (large, flat stones used for religious rituals) from

Mesoamerica

Mesoamerica, meaning *middle America*, is on the isthmus (a strip of land with water on two sides) that joins North and South America. Today, this area includes present-day southern and central Mexico, the Yucatán Peninsula, and the northern parts of Central America (Guatemala, northern Honduras and El Salvador). Meso-american borders were not fixed in the same way we think of borders today, because *Mesoamerican* refers not just to a geographic region but also to a shared cultural tradition.

Throughout ancient Mesoamerica there were many different language groups. However, the peoples shared religious beliefs, a calendar with the same basic structure, and methods of food production and preparation. Some examples of specific ideas they shared are blood-letting (ceremonial withdrawing of blood), ceramic lip plugs (decorative ornaments that pierce the lip), decapitators (wooden swords edged with stone blades used to behead people), quilted cotton breastplates (armor to cover the chest), sandals with heels, and a ball game played in ceremonial courts with a solid rubber ball.

the giant basalt blocks they cut from hardened lava. The Olmecs carved monumental thrones, as well; some of these may have been refashioned into heads after the death of the ruler. Later, the Maya also carved stelae and altars, sometimes in a style similar to the Olmec. One motif (reoccurring artistic theme) common to both the Olmecs and the Maya was a carving of a ruler seated inside a gaping mouth. The mouth symbolized the cave-like entrance to the underworld.

Mesoamerican cultures were influenced by the Olmecs, and also influenced them. What emerged is a group of "sister" cultures that shared many elements, including art and architecture. This shared Olmec culture can be seen in designs for buildings where public ceremonies were held, residences for the elite (persons of the highest class), and houses for commoners. They also shared ideas about mythology, kingship, and class hierarchy (a system where people are ranked one above the other). The products people valued and trade routes throughout Mesoamerica also grew out of a shared Olmec culture. This continued long after the Olmecs disappeared in the middle of the Preclassic Era.

THE MAYA IN THE PRECLASSIC ERA

In the Middle Preclassic Period (ca. 1000–400 B.C.E.), Maya chiefdoms emerged. The first ones appeared throughout the Pacific coast and the highlands in the south. By this time, these expanding settlements were linked by trade routes that ran from modern-day Mexico to Central America.

As populations grew, the Maya area divided into many rival chiefdoms, each with its own capital city and king. The number of kings competing for power grew from a few dozen to as many as 60 at the height of Maya civilization.

These chiefdoms were villages ruled by a small group of powerful elites. Villagers believed the chief had supernatural powers that enabled him (or, on rare occasions, her) to appeal to the gods on their behalf. In return, the chief accepted tribute (tax paid to a ruler) in the form of goods from his people. He used this tribute for personal use, and also in rituals and to form alliances with neighboring chiefs.

To keep pace with the increases in population, construction increased too. More buildings were being constructed, and these buildings were larger. Platforms of stone or adobe (mud that is hardened into a building material by drying it in the sun) that served as the foundations for temples and the houses of the elite soared higher and higher.

Some time around 400 B.C.E., Maya rulers began to record their reign by having their portraits carved into stone monuments. The carvings showed the rulers wearing ceremonial masks and headdresses, which was evidence of their connection to the gods. Plazas were constructed to display the monuments. Some plazas had many stelae lined up side-by-side like giant dominoes, recording a royal dynasty (a sequence of rulers from the same family). Each monument was carved with pictures and symbols that showed the king's story—his political and religious authority, his achievements as a brave warrior, and his place among the gods.

Maya Dates

Accurately dating events that happened 3,000 years ago or more can be difficult. Converting dates on the Maya Long Count calendar to dates on the modern calendar has given rise to disagreements among historians. This is true even when they look at Spanish accounts of Maya history (which use the modern calendar) and astronomical events such as new moons and eclipses.

Dates given for rulers in this book follow a convention known as the Goodman-Martinez-Thompson correlation, or GMT. This is a widely accepted system among scholars that relates the Long Count to the modern calendar. The GMT also matches the sacred 260-day calendar that the Maya in Guatemala continue to use today.

The early Maya, like all peoples, were attracted to the best real estate. They favored fertile soil for growing plants, plentiful rainfall for healthy crops, and land close to valued resources such as obsidian. Each territory had access to different resources, such as farmland, brilliant quetzal (a Central American bird) feathers, or jade. Because no territory had everything, some communities tried to dominate others. This led to warfare.

Warfare played an important role in the development of Maya civilization. Rulers armed with fierce weapons led attacks against their rivals. A ruler's power and importance depended on his skill and success as a warrior. The winners gained control over larger territories, populations, and trade routes. Important captives, such as the ruler of a conquered Maya city, were ritually sacrificed. This increased the conquering ruler's status. Sometimes elite individuals would be buried with the heads of their enemies that they had taken as battle trophies.

IN THEIR OWN WORDS

The Records of the 13th King

Beautifully carved stelae grace the grand plazas of the ancient Maya city of Copán, located in present-day western Honduras. The monument archaeologists call Stela 1 shows the king with all of his ceremonial clothing and objects. He is shown in a place called Macaw Mountain, which may be one of the sacred hills around Copán.

The stela commemorates dates that have special significance to the Maya people and the ceremonies the king carried out on those important dates. (A *k'atun* is equal to 7,200 days or slightly less than 20 years.) From the top, it reads:

> It was erected [the stone].
> It is the image of the Macaw Mountain Lord.
> It ended the 15 k'atuns.
> He casts incense.
> He is the impersonator [of a deity].

The end of the inscription says he is the 13th successor in the dynasty. Then it gives his personal name, Uaxac Lahun Ubac C'awil.

(Source: "Lost King of the Maya." Nova Online. Available online. URL: http://www.pbs.org/wgbh/nova/maya/copa_transcript.html#11. Accessed October 13, 2008.)

KAMINALJUYÚ AND THE HIGHLANDS

One of the earliest centers of complex society emerged in Kaminaljuyú (the name means "place of the ancient ones" in Mayan). The city lies just west of modern Guatemala City on a flat, fertile plateau (an area of high, flat ground). Maya builders constructed earthen mounds—platforms that supported buildings made of wood, plaster, and thatch (a roof covering made of palm fronds). They built monuments and tombs.

Although Kaminaljuyú was occupied in the Early Preclassic Period more than 3,000 years ago, it did not become an important power until the Middle Preclassic Period. By the Late Preclassic Period, it was the dominant city in the highlands area.

Rulers at Kaminaljuyú gained status not only from religion and warfare, but also from water management. In 600 B.C.E., the Maya at Kaminaljuyú dug a series of irrigation canals that brought water from Lake Miraflores to their planted fields. These canals were an engineering feat. They carried massive quantities of water from the lake to maize fields five miles away, in canals 60 feet wide and 26 feet deep.

The irrigation canals brought water to a number of important crops. For example, cacao was cultivated for its seeds, which were used to make cocoa and chocolate, and rubber was used by the Maya to make balls for their games.

Kaminaljuyú owed much of its wealth to the nearby volcanoes. The frequent eruptions spewed ash that enriched the soil. And the underground heat created obsidian, which was a valuable trade item. Much of Kaminaljuyú's importance came from the fact that it controlled the quarrying and export of obsidian and jade.

In the fifth century, Kaminaljuyú began trading with cities in central Mexico. With no wheels or large animals to carry heavy loads, humans carried jade and obsidian over land to trade with other communities. They also lugged mica (a sparkly mineral that Maya artists used like glitter on everything from masks to buildings) and hematite and cinnabar, two mineral pigments used to create color.

One thing Kaminaljuyú lacked was building stone. With no quarries nearby, the builders could not construct stone pyramids and platforms, although they did create some carved stone monuments. But Kaminaljuyú's platforms were made from clay and its temples were

Kaminaljuyú lacked building stone, and so many of its great buildings were made of clay bricks that have since washed away. But the residents did have enough stone to make monuments such as this one, which shows a male figure dancing.

made from wood, mud plaster, and thatch—all materials that did not survive the centuries. Of the structures that did survive, most were bulldozed when modern Guatemala City expanded. And so Kaminaljuyú's true urban plan will remain a mystery.

The lack of building stone did not mean that Kaminaljuyú was a poor city. From the rich grave goods found in the royal tombs, it is clear that Kaminaljuyú's elite lived a life of luxury. Archaeologists have found the remains of an important Kaminaljuyú residence surrounded by treasures, many of which were made from jade.

Although no one city ever dominated the entire Maya area, Kaminaljuyú grew to be the largest Preclassic ceremonial center in the Maya highlands. Kaminaljuyú was on the brink of becoming what scholars define as a state when, at the end of the Preclassic Era, Lake Miraflores dried up. This had been the source of water for the Kaminaljuyú irrigation canals. The once-flowing canals filled with silt (fine sand carried by moving water and deposited as sediment). In what was to become a pattern for the Maya, this center declined, while other population centers in the Maya area took root and flourished.

THE LOWLANDS

During the Middle Preclassic Period, Maya villagers followed the rivers inland and began to colonize (migrate to an area and settle in) the lowlands. As populations grew, the number of settlements increased and people moved into the rainforest regions of the lowlands.

Like the people in the highlands, the lowlands Maya built thatched-roofed shelters around a central courtyard. Some villages included a larger platform where public gatherings, religious ceremonies, and community activities could be performed.

In what is today the Petén region of Guatemala, a site called Nakbé grew quickly during the Preclassic Era because of the people's efficient farming practices. They made elevated garden plots, called terraces, enclosed with stone walls. Then they enriched the soil by adding nutrient-rich earth from nearby marshlands. Linda Schele and David Freidel wrote in *A Forest of Kings*, "Excavating the muck at the bottom of the swamps to create a system of raised fields and canals took organization of time and labor. The result was worth the effort. . . . The bottom mud became loaded with nutrients from fish excretions, thus providing rich fertilizer for the fields."

The Maya were learning how to get the most out of their land. They were creating more farmland by enriching the soil in Nakbé and providing water to otherwise unusable land by digging irrigation canals in Kaminaljuyú. These practices enabled the land to support larger populations. But with each jump in population size, the gap between life as a farmer and life as a ruler widened.

EL MIRADOR IN THE CENTRAL LOWLANDS

Despite Nakbé's head start as one of the earliest cities in the region, it fell behind the rapidly growing polity (an organized society with a system of government) of El Mirador, just seven miles away. El Mirador ("the lookout" in Spanish) was the most powerful city in the lowlands during the Late Preclassic Period. It flourished as a trading center between 300 B.C.E. and 150 C.E. Smaller lowlands communities ended up becoming El Mirador's ally or being conquered by it.

If there is one word to describe El Mirador, it would be *big*. Everything about El Mirador was big. In its time, it was the largest city in the entire Maya area and one of the largest in all of Mesoamerica. The ceremonial center sprawled for almost a mile east to west. Plazas at El Mirador were large enough to hold thousands of people assembled to watch rituals performed by the elite. Plazas were used not only for ceremonies, but also as public markets.

El Mirador has the largest temples ever built by the Maya. One is probably the largest pyramid in the world—larger at its base than the Great Pyramid in Egypt. Its base covers an area bigger than 36 football fields.

A multitude of craftsmen contributed to building this massive metropolis—astronomers, architects, engineers, artists, carpenters, stonemasons, and laborers. Astronomers positioned important buildings to align with the movements of the Sun and the Moon. Builders dressed the buildings in stone and artists decorated them with stucco masks depicting gods and kings.

The enormous scale of the buildings at El Mirador shows the power of those who ruled this ceremonial center deep in the jungle. The kings of El Mirador were as powerful as the great pharaohs of Egypt. At its peak, El Mirador was home to as many as 100,000 people who worked not only as builders, but also as farmers, priests, warriors, and merchants. To feed this enormous population, hunters supplemented what

The Giant Pyramid

The huge pyramid at El Mirador rises nearly 260 feet in three stages. The first platform is 23 feet high and 1,000 feet on each side. This platform supports several buildings. The second, smaller platform also rises 23 feet and is the foundation for a third platform that soars 70 feet. Finally, perched on top, is an immense pyramid known as La Danta.

Gene and George Stuart wrote in *Lost Kingdoms of the Maya* that giant buildings like this served as symbols of larger objects, "pyramids as mountains, and temples as caves leading to the Underworld, their doorways made in the image of gaping monster mouths."

Raised Roads

One large feature of El Mirador was the causeways (raised roads) that linked the Mirador Basin communities. These roads ran outward from El Mirador's center. Some rose 12 feet high and stretched more than 150 feet wide. The causeways were an ambitious major construction project for a people who had no wagons, carts, or any wheeled vehicles.

the farmer grew with the meat from turkeys, deer, dogs, wild pigs, and reptiles such as iguanas and turtles.

Traders and merchants set up their wares in open-air stalls in the city's large plazas. Merchants supplied El Mirador's citizens with exotic trade goods such as jade, obsidian, shells, and salt. The people of El Mirador and neighboring cities traveled to these markets on causeways that radiated out from the center of the city, connecting important areas within the city and nearby cities under El Mirador's rule, such as Nakbé, Wakná, and Tintal.

The people of El Mirador and the lowlands associated power with the supernatural world. This was different from the Maya in the southern highlands, who at first associated power with their kings. Artists in the lowlands decorated ceremonial centers with carved masks of gods and symbols of the gods' supernatural realm. But in the highlands, artists decorated ceremonial centers with carved stelae commemorating kings and the achievements of their reigns. Eventually, these two practices blended. Lowland polities continued to build enormous temples as stages for their rulers to perform rituals to the supernatural, but they also built monuments recording those rulers' worldly deeds.

The massive cities throughout the Mirador Basin, including El Mirador, were abandoned around 150–400 C.E. It was not until the Late Classic Period that a much smaller population reoccupied El Mirador. Among the Maya who lived there in 700 C.E. were groups of talented scribes (people who write down official documents) and potters. These artists developed a style of ceramics unique to the Mirador Basin consisting of black line drawings against a cream-colored ceramic background.

DECLINE ENDS THE PRECLASSIC ERA

Mayanists do not agree about what caused people to leave El Mirador or about the general Maya decline, which came between 150 and 250. Richard Hanson, an archaeologist from the University of California at Los Angeles, believes the downfall of El Mirador could have been the result of an ecological disaster caused by making so much plaster for the extensive building projects. In a 1995 article in the *New York Times* ("Did Maya Doom Themselves By Felling Trees?" written by

William H. Honan) Hanson said, "You have to burn about 20 big trees and all their branches in order to make only a little pile of lime about one meter high. So they hacked down forests. The deforestation led to soil erosion and that filled in the seasonal swamps where they had been collecting peat to fertilize their terraced agricultural gardens. They messed in their nest and made these areas uninhabitable."

Hanson said using up resources this way was also a characteristic of the larger Maya decline centuries later. But not all scientists agree. David Freidel, professor of archaeology at Southern Methodist University in Dallas, said in the same article that the greater decline was due to nonstop warfare that "lasted 400 years, leading to anarchic violence and pure chaos."

Many archaeologists do not believe there was one single cause. They attribute the decline to a variety of factors. In the same article, Maya archaeologist Jeremy Sadloff says, "You must consider population pressure on the agricultural system, constant warfare, changing trade routes, and the possibility of drought and other climatic factors."

Whatever the cause of the decline that marked the end of the Preclassic Era, Robert J. Sharer concludes in *The Ancient Maya*, "The downfall of Preclassic Maya civilization paved the way for the rebirth of a host of new state-level polities that dominated the lowland landscape in the Classic Era."

The potters who lived in El Mirador during the Late Classic Period developed a unique style of ceramics featuring black lines against a light background. This pot shows a scribe learning his craft.

CHAPTER 2

THE CLASSIC ERA: RISE AND FALL OF THE SUPERPOWERS

SCHOLARS DIVIDE THE CLASSIC ERA OF MAYA CIVILIZATION into three periods. In the Early Classic Period (ca. 250–600), a series of cities in the southern lowlands expanded and flourished, making that area the center of Maya power. During the Late Classic Period (ca. 600–800), populations in the cities of the southern lowlands reached their peak. New city-states also rose to prominence. The Terminal Classic Period (ca. 800–900) is marked by the decline of the city-states in the southern lowlands, while in the Yucatán and the highlands new cities rose.

OPPOSITE

The Great Plaza in Tikal was surrounded by grand palaces and temples. This is Temple I.

TIKAL: SUPERPOWER OF THE LOWLANDS

When El Mirador declined at the end of the Preclassic Era, it opened the door for many smaller polities in the lowlands to expand into powerful cities ruled by divine kings. Several superpowers emerged. George and Gene Stuart wrote about one of these superpowers, called Tikal, in *Lost Kingdoms of the Maya:* "Tikal was enormous. Its six-square-mile central zone holds some 3,000 visible constructions—wide causeways linking major groups of temples, pyramids, palaces, shrines, ball courts, plazas, house sites, and even ritual sweathouses. As many as 10,000 earlier platforms and buildings may lie beneath the surface. The ancient residential zone sprawls over more than 23 square miles of forest."

The Long Count Calendar

From the second to the 10th century, the Maya used a fixed date calendar to record significant dates. Mayanists call this calendar the Long Count. In addition to the Long Count, the Maya also had a sacred calendar, used by priests for divination (predicting the future), that was cyclical (when the cycle was finished, it began again). This kind of calendar makes it difficult to pinpoint when a specific event occurred, such as a king's ascent to the throne.

Modern calendars are fixed date calendars like the Long Count. Each day in a modern calendar happens only once. So, for example, once April 28, 2008, has passed, it will never come again.

For the Maya, the very first day was 13.0.0.0.0 4 Ahaw 8 Kumk'u. By the calendar used today, this would be August 11, 3114 B.C.E. This method of tracking dates has proved useful to archaeologists, who now can match Long Count dates and the historic events associated with them to the modern calendar.

Bringing Water to Tikal

With no water sources in the immediate area, Tikal's first building priority was water management. By damming and plastering natural ravines, the Maya of Tikal were able to collect and store rainwater in large reservoirs called *aguadas*. The entire central portion of Tikal is surrounded by very large *aguadas*.

Tikal ("place of the voices" in Mayan) was the largest Classic Era city in the southern lowlands. Hieroglyphic inscriptions show that the Maya who lived there called their city Yax Mutul ("first hair knot") and the kingdom as a whole Mutul ("hair knot"). For more than 1,000 years, the Maya continued to build at Tikal.

In the second century B.C.E., the Maya of Tikal built the Great Plaza by leveling a large area, laying limestone, and then finishing the surface with plaster. Surrounding the Great Plaza they built the North Acropolis, a ceremonial center, the Central Acropolis, a 700-foot long palace, and Temple I and Temple II—two great temples dedicated to the great jaguar and the Moon. Tikal's eight largest pyramids, some 20 stories high, are surrounded by many more impressive structures. Temple IV is the tallest pyramid at Tikal and in the Maya area, at about 230 feet tall. It was probably built between 734 and 766.

The people of Tikal were perhaps the first Maya to record the bloodline of their kings. They carved these records in stone monuments. From them, historians know that Tikal was ruled by a line of 39 kings in a single dynasty that spanned 800 years.

Although he was not the first ruler of Tikal, the king the Maya recognized as their dynasty's founder was First Step Shark (Yax Ehb Xook). None of First Step Shark's monuments remains. Scholars must estimate the dates of his reign based on the sequence of rulers carved on later monuments by his descendants. Many scholars place his reign at about 100.

First Step Shark must have been a powerful king, because his people gave him the title of founder of a dynasty. He may have gained this respect from his skill on the battlefield or by being the first to lead Tikal to political independence. First Step Shark's long line of descendants ruled Tikal and formed the elite community of its royal court.

The earliest date carved into a monument at Tikal is 8.12.14.8.15 in the Maya Long Count calendar, which is the year 292. The monument portrays ruler Scroll Ahau Jaguar (?-B'alam, dates unknown) in full kingly dress. Although the carving style the Maya artists used is similar to earlier Olmec monuments, there are details that would become typically Maya for centuries to come. The king is surrounded by emblems that declare his rank and power. He holds a double-headed serpent bar from which the human-headed form of the sun god emerges. This symbol of Maya royalty shows the king's connection to the gods and his ability to bring them from the supernatural world into the real world.

TIKAL CONQUERS UAXACTÚN

No more than a day's walk north of Tikal, another polity, Uaxactún (*wah-shak-TOON*), was growing and began competing with Tikal for resources. Like Tikal, Uaxactún entered the Classic Era prosperous and powerful. Also like Tikal, its early historical records are spotty and incomplete. The monuments at Uaxactún are similar in design to those found at Tikal, though, and suggest that the kings of Uaxactún were also both warriors and kings.

Both polities competed for local power and resources. During the reign of Tikal's king Great Jaguar Paw (Chak Tok Ich'aak I, r. 360–378), the competition between Uaxactún and Tikal came to a head. The conflict marked a turning point in Maya warfare. No longer was it enough for Great Jaguar Paw to take captives in battle. Now he was after an entire kingdom.

What Is His Name?

Mayanists have not yet been able to translate all of the Maya glyphs. There is also some uncertainty about which kings ruled and when—particularly because several have the same name. Sometimes, Mayanists will know what a king's name means in English but not fully know what the Mayan sounded like. Scholars deal with words they do not know, or areas of uncertainty, by adding numbers or question marks to the way they write some names in Mayan.

Teotihuacan, the City of the Gods

Around the time of Christ, Teotihuacan (*tay-o-tee-HWA-kahn*), located just northeast of present-day Mexico City, grew to be the largest urban center in the Americas. In fact, it was as large as any city anywhere in the world. It is not known what Teotihuacan's people called their city-state, but centuries after its fall the Aztec people named it Teotihuacan, meaning "city of the gods."

The Aztecs believed the pyramids along Teotihuacan's central boulevard were tombs, so they named the roadway Avenue of the Dead. Today's scholars know that these impressive pyramids were actually ceremonial platforms where the elite of Teotihuacan performed dramatic public rituals.

Teotihuacan is a prime example of urban planning. There are more than 2,000 structures. Building them required engineering more advanced than anything found in Europe at that time.

Tikal and Teotihuacan traded goods such as green obsidian, pottery, and most importantly—ideas. In Tikal and Uaxactún, monuments and murals show the Maya rulers greeting ambassadors from Teotihuacan in a submissive way. Scholars can only speculate about what tensions existed between the great polities.

Teotihuacan met its end in the eighth century, when it was burned and destroyed by unknown invaders. Over time, the jungle engulfed what was once the greatest city in the world.

A member of the Tikal royal family named Smoking Frog (Siyaj K'ak', dates unknown) led Tikal's warriors into battle against Uaxactún. That is because the king, Great Jaguar Paw, died just when Smoking Frog arrived. Smoking Frog probably had strong ties to the great city-state of Teotihuacan, although scholars think he was Maya.

In 378, Smoking Frog conquered the Uaxactún. With his conquest, Tikal became the dominant polity in the central Petén region. Artists commemorated this occasion by carving a monument showing Smoking Frog in full warrior costume, gripping a club with an obsidian blade club. This image is the earliest found so far that commemorates conquest.

Smoking Frog ruled in Uaxactún as second-in-command under Great Jaguar Paw's successor in Tikal, Curl Snout (Yax Nuun Ayiin I,

r. 379–404). But monuments suggest that Smoking Frog was really the one in charge.

Curl Snout remained in power for about 30 years. During that time, he maintained close connections with rulers from Teotihuacan in central Mexico, and also had some contact with rulers from Kaminaljuyú in the highlands. These trade and military alliances between Tikal and other major centers strengthened Tikal's importance in the region.

One by one, the smaller polities around Tikal stopped erecting monuments to their own rulers. Robert Sharer writes in *Daily Life in Maya Civilization* that this was "a sure sign that Tikal had taken them over by warfare or alliance. In war, the defeated ruler was sacrificed and a puppet ruler took his place. In alliance, the local ruler acknowledged the supremacy of the Tikal king, an event usually commemorated by the exchange of royal brides from the ruling families of each city."

CALAKMUL CLASHES WITH TIKAL

Calakmul, a massive complex in the lowlands, got its modern name from the biologist who discovered the site in 1931. In Mayan, *ca* means "two," *lak* means "adjacent" (next to), and *mul* means "mound" or "pyramid." So Calakmul means the City of the Two Adjacent Pyramids. But the ancient Maya called their city Kaan ("snake"). To them, it was the Kingdom of the Snake.

Calakmul was fortunate to be near many bodies of water. The ancient Maya turned these into reservoirs to irrigate their crops and supply drinking water. Their water management techniques supported a large population. There were as many as 50,000 city residents. Including the rural residents living in the outskirts of the city, that number rose in the Late Classic Period to as high as 100,000.

Calakmul was an important city from the Late Preclassic Period until 909. It was the most powerful city in the lowlands during the seventh century. Calakmul expanded its influence by forming alliances with neighboring cities through marriages. But its constant conflict with Tikal eventually led to its downfall.

Tikal and Calakmul controlled the trade along the rivers in their respective areas. And both dominated the overland routes in their regions as well. Tikal's conquest of Río Azul to the northeast may have threatened Calakmul's dominion and sparked a series of wars. Or it may

Making War by the Stars
Throughout much of Mesoamerica, battles were timed to the movements of the planets, especially Venus. A favorite time to attack was during the first appearance of Venus as the evening star.

Caracol

The first archaeologist who visited Caracol in the southern lowlands after its discovery in 1937 noticed a large number of snails clinging to the walls of the ruined buildings. So he named the city *caracol,* which means "snail" in Spanish. In overall area, Caracol is one of the largest ancient Maya cities. During its height in the Classic Era, the city covered 19 square miles and was home to more than 120,000 people. At 138 feet, Caracol's tallest building, Caana ("sky place"), is the tallest building in Belize—past and present.

More than 22 miles of causeways radiated from Caracol's ceremonial center like spokes on a wheel. They connected the center to its agricultural areas and suburbs. Some suburban areas appear to have been residential areas for the elite, with solid construction and causeways leading directly into the center. Not all of the structures in the suburbs were residential. Causeways sometimes led to administrative hubs and centers for market trade. Archaeologists call these the strip malls of the past.

Although Caracol entered a century-long period of decline in 680, it was experiencing a revival and undergoing extensive rebuilding when it suddenly collapsed in 895. People continued to live and work in the suburbs after the city was burned and abandoned at the end of the ninth century.

have been unavoidable that these two titans would clash. The Petén region just may not have been big enough for the both of them.

During the Early Classic Period, Calakmul began a campaign to cut Tikal off from its trade partners. Sky Witness (u-?-?-Chan, r. ca. 561–572), the king of Calakmul, did this by making alliances with the cities that surrounded Tikal. Once Tikal was encircled by hostile polities, Sky Witness planned to make his move.

When Caracol's king, Lord Water (Yajaw Te'k'inich II, r. 553–593), switched alliances from Tikal to Calakmul, it was too much for the king of Tikal, Double Bird (Wak Chan K'awiil, r. 537–562). He sought revenge by attacking Caracol.

In 562, Double Bird was captured and sacrificed by the king of Caracol. With Tikal crippled, Calakmul stepped in and defeated Tikal. The victors smashed and defaced Tikal's monuments. Double Bird's descendants were forced to submit to Calakmul's rule. Any wealth they had now belonged to Calakmul.

A once thriving population began to shrink. The people of Tikal were no longer safe in their own territory, and outlying villagers were forced to move into the city center for safety. For the next 150 years, Tikal spiraled downward while Calakmul and Caracol experienced growth and prosperity.

Despite Calakmul's new status in the region, it was unable to dominate its allies surrounding Tikal. The polities not only maintained their independence, but enjoyed an expansion of their own now that Tikal had no power.

THE LATE CLASSIC PERIOD: TIKAL'S ROYALTY LOOKS ELSEWHERE

After Tikal's defeat, the polities that surrounded it grew and expanded. In 629, Tikal's king K'inich Mwaan Jol II (dates unknown), founded a new colony west of Tikal, known today as Dos Pilas. He set up his toddler son, Flint Sky (B'alaj Chan K'awiil, r. 648–692), as its ruler.

Dos Pilas lay in a water-rich region of Guatemala called Petexbatún. It was established to be an ally and colony of Tikal, in hopes of fending off attacks from Calakmul. However, Tikal's king and Flint Sky were defeated by Calakmul in 648. K'inich Mwaan Jol II may have died in the battle.

By now, Flint Sky was in his early 20s. He realized that his budding city was vulnerable. To flourish in his new city, he would need support. So he broke with his family in Tikal and allied himself with Calakmul.

From this point forward, Calakmul used Dos Pilas to attack Tikal and other polities. Using cleverness and aggression, Flint Sky soon became a rising political and military power of the Maya lowlands. In 672, the new king of Tikal, Flint Sky's brother Shield Skull (Nuun Ujol Chaak, r. 657–679), attacked Dos Pilas and gained control of the colony. He sent Flint Sky into exile.

Flint Sky called on his ally, Calakmul, for help. In 677, Calakmul attacked and defeated Tikal once again and Flint Sky was returned to the throne in Dos Pilas. In 679, Flint Sky and

CONNECTIONS

Plenty of Water

In April and May, at the end of the dry season in the Maya lowlands, water is scarce. Ancient residents were forced to come up with water management solutions. The large population in Calakmul required a great deal of water for their farms and for personal use. They solved the problem of shortages by digging at least five major reservoirs to serve the city. One rectangular reservoir measures 800 by 700 feet, making it the largest in all the Maya area. During the rainy season, rivers as well as rain water feed these reservoirs.

Modern archaeologists conduct their field research during the dry season. One major challenge for any excavation is carrying in enough water to support a large team. At Calakmul, archaeologists are relieved of that burden. They use the ancient Maya reservoirs for their water supply.

Husbands and Wives

Marriage ceremonies were rarely commemorated on Maya monuments. In fact, the terms "wife" and "husband" almost never appeared in Mayan inscriptions. Queens were identified in terms of the heirs (sons in line to become king) they provided for the kingdom. One exception was a king of Yaxchilán, Bird Jaguar III (Yaxum Balam, r. 629–669). It is likely that the reason Bird Jaguar's wives are mentioned prominently on monuments is because his marriages were arranged as political alliances. It was the custom in Mesoamerica to take royal brides from conquered cities as symbols of the new order.

his Calakmul ally went to war against his brother Shield Skull at Tikal. Shield Skull was captured and eventually sacrificed.

In 698, Shield God K (Itzamnaaj K'awiil, r. 698–726) became the king of Dos Pilas. Like Flint Sky, he focused on expanding Dos Pilas. Through marriage and conquest, the rulers of Dos Pilas continued to boost their city's prestige in the region. Dos Pilas remained an independent polity allied with Calakmul. Meanwhile, the descendants of Shield Skull were plotting their revenge.

Eventually, Tikal became strong enough to once again threaten Dos Pilas. The warriors of Dos Pilas scrambled to build a defensive wall to protect their city. They grabbed stones from every source available—temple platforms, residences, even the royal palace. They built walls over sacred sites. One wall sits atop staircases whose inscriptions illustrate the history of Dos Pilas.

But their efforts failed. In 761, Dos Pilas fell to Tikal. Some members of the ruling elite must have sensed that their rule was weakening, because a year before Dos Pilas's collapse, they fled.

Unrest within the Petexbatún region never stopped. Cities were transformed into fortresses, with people digging moats for protection and building walls. Everything needed protecting—not only town centers, but farms and fields as well. Ultimately, warfare was the region's undoing. Most of the population fled to safer territories, nearly abandoning the entire Petexbatún region.

YAXCHILÁN

Another group of polities west of the Petexbatún region reached their highest point during the Late Classic Period. Along the Usumacinta River there is a spot where the river loops back on itself. Inside the loop, Yaxchilán grew powerful, protected by the natural barricade provided by the river.

Three Jaguar kings ruled Yaxchilán for a prosperous period of 175 years: Shield Jaguar II (Itzamnaaj B'alam II, r. 681–742), Bird Jaguar IV (Yaxum Balam IV, r. 752–768), and Shield Jaguar III (Itzamnaaj B'alam III, r. 769–800). Yaxchilán had once been an ally of Tikal, and suffered the consequences of supporting the losing side. But Yaxchilán bounced back—although scholars are not sure why. In fact, Yaxchilán recovered so well that it dominated the Usumacinta region until the end of the Late Classic Period.

Bird Jaguar IV, king of Yaxchilán, is shown in full warrior dress with a spear in his right hand. A captive sits at his feet.

TIKAL'S DOWNFALL

Ruler A (Hasaw Chan K'awiil I, r. 682–734), Tikal's 26th ruler, attempted to return his city to its former glory. Ruler A stirred his people by reminding them of Tikal's golden years. He began by honoring past distinguished kings. He recovered King Stormy Sky's (Siyan Chan K'awiil II, r. 411–456) monument and moved it to a rear room in Stormy Sky's funerary temple. He then had a new and grander temple built on top of the old one. Ruler A also buried Jaguar Paw Skull's (Chak Tok Ich'aak II, r. ca. 486–508) broken monument with great ceremony.

Once proper respect had been paid to Ruler A's ancestors, he plotted revenge on Tikal's enemies. Ruler A chipped away at Calakmul's power by raiding its allies—copying the strategy Calakmul had

Piedras Negras Holds the Key

The largest city in the string of polities along the Usumacinta River was Piedras Negras, located 25 miles downriver from Yaxchilán. Piedras Negras is known for its beautiful monuments. Archaeologists excavating the city in the 1930s uncovered a royal tomb and structures designed for the elite. Archaeologists excavating in the 1990s uncovered farmers' residences.

The inscriptions carved into Piedras Negras's many monuments provided an important key to unlocking the secrets of Mayan hieroglyphic writing. It became clear from the texts on the monuments at Piedras Negras that inscriptions were not only about astronomical events and mythical subjects, as scholars previously thought. The inscriptions also made references to political history. Once scholars understood that they were looking at a historical record, they were able to slowly unravel the glyphs' meanings.

One of the early glyphs that was understood by modern scholars was "accession to power." This, associated with a date, marked the inauguration of a king. Other glyphs whose meanings were discovered from monuments at Piedras Negras included the symbols for birth and death.

once used to weaken Tikal. Then, in 695, Ruler A invaded Calakmul. Ruler A captured Calakmul's king, Jaguar Paw (Yuknoom Yich'aak, r. ca. 686–695), tortured him for 40 days, then sacrificed him to the gods.

Ruler A ruled for 50 years. When he died, he was buried with all the magnificence a king of his great stature deserved.

Ruler A's son, Ruler B (Yik'in Chan K'awiil, r. 734–760), was one of Tikal's greatest kings. He defeated many of Calakmul's rivals and, eventually, Calakmul itself. He also built Tikal's largest pyramid, Temple IV, and added onto and rebuilt much of the city center.

Ruler B's sons and grandsons, however, ruled with mixed success. Chitam (Yasaw Chan K'awiil II, dates unknown), Tikal's 33rd and last ruler, was probably either a great-grandson or a great-great-grandson of Ruler A. He failed to realize the vision of his ancestors. In 869, when Tikal's last monument was raised, Tikal was already doomed. The ancient city broke into small communities and was covered over by the jungle.

PALENQUE IN THE WEST

Palenque, in the western region of the lowlands, had a long string of rulers who came from three dynasties. The most likely founder of the first dynasty is Jaguar Quetzal (K'uk' B'alam I, r. ca. 431–435). In 583, the last king in this dynasty died. Because he had no male heirs, Lady Olnal (r. 583–604) became his successor. She was the first woman to rule Palenque.

Maya women were not allowed to marry people within their father's family. So Lady Olnal married a man from outside her family line. Therefore, her son, Ac Kan (Ah Ne Ol Mat, r. 605–612), marked a break in the first dynasty when he became king in 605.

When Ac Kan died, Palenque had been soundly defeated by Calakmul and was at an all-time low. Ac Kan had no son, and so the royal line was again broken. Lady Sak K'uk (r. 612–615), the daughter of Ac Kan's brother, took the throne. She took the name Muwaan Mat—the name of the goddess who gave birth to three gods that were special to Palenque.

She ruled for only three years while her son, Hanab Pakal (r. 615–683), grew old enough to become king. When Hanab Pakal took the throne at 12 years old, he marked the beginning of a new dynasty in Palenque.

Hanab Pakal ruled for 67 years and brought prosperity to Palenque. He expended a great deal of energy honoring the gods and carving creation myths on monuments. These actions raised his own prestige. His efforts were meant to prove his right to rule, even though he was not from the family line of the founding dynasty. Hanab Pakal also claimed there was a connection between his mother and the goddess known as First Mother. This association conveniently made Hanab Pakal a descendant of the gods. From Hanab Pakal's reign forward, the Palenque kings did not just claim they had a special relationship with the gods. They claimed they were directly descended from the gods.

Hanab Pakal lived a long life. This meant that his son, Kan Balam (K'inich Kan B'alam II, r. 684–702), was middle-aged by the time he stepped up to the throne. Kan Balam ruled for 18 years. When he died in 702, his younger brother, Kan Xul (K'inich K'an Hoy Chitam II, r. 702–711), took over.

Kan Xul's reign was full of trouble. He built an addition onto the royal residence, and needed captives to sacrifice for the dedication ceremonies. So he raided his neighbor city, Toniná. But things did

Canoeing to the Underworld

In a dark corner of Ruler A's tomb, modern archaeologists found a bundle of bones—90 in all. Carved in the bones were scenes of Ruler A taking his last canoe voyages into the waters of the underworld. Old Jaguar God and Aged Stingray Spine God paddle from the front and back, while Ruler A occupies the center of the canoe with animal co-passengers on the trip to the underworld—iguana, spider monkey, parrot, and dog. The bone image is inscribed: "Ruler A canoed four *k'atuns* to his passing" (quoted in Linda Schele and Mary Ellen Miller's *The Blood of Kings*). This means Ruler A lived 80 years until his death.

This figure of Hanab Pakal was found in a tomb at Palenque.

not go as planned. Kan Xul was captured instead. Without a king, Palenque struggled.

As long as the king of Toniná kept Kan Xul alive, the people of Palenque could not replace him with a new king. The king of Toniná kept Kan Xul captive for years. Finally, probably in 721, he was sacrificed.

After Kan Xul was sacrificed, a series of kings in Palenque ruled over the gradual decline of royal authority. Finally, in 799, Palenque recorded the accession of its last king, Pakal III, and then quietly disappeared from the records.

COPÁN IN THE SOUTHEAST

Copán dominated the southeastern Maya area through a long, unbroken line of 16 rulers. The ruler who founded the dynasty in 426 was Yax Kuk Mo (K'inich Yax K'uk'mo', r. ca. 426–437).

Two kings had exceptionally long reigns. This provided Copán with the stability that enabled it to blossom. The kings were Smoking Sky (B'utz' Chan, r. 578–628), who ruled for 50 years, and Smoke Imix (K'ak' Nab K'awiil, r. 628–695), who ruled for 67 years.

Copán's rich resources supported its growth during this period of stability. The polity was located on fertile agricultural lands. It was also strategically positioned on important trade routes. During Smoke Imix's reign, Copán's population increased dramatically and the city sprawled outward over the valley.

When 18 Rabbit (Waxaklahun Ub'ah K'awiil, r. 695–738) became ruler after Smoke Imix died in 695, Copán went through a construction phase. The Great Plaza, an open place like a square and surrounded on all four sides by buildings, was refurbished. King 18 Rabbit claimed that Copán was as great as the Classic Era cities Tikal, Palenque, and

Calakmul. But his construction projects were cut short when he was captured and beheaded by a neighboring lord.

As a result, Copán fell on hard times. It was not long before Copán lost control over its agricultural lands and trade routes. It took the efforts of Smoke Shell (K'ak' Yipyaj Chan K'awiil, r. 749–761), Copán's 15th king, to revitalize Copán.

One of Smoke Shell's most outstanding contributions was building the Hieroglyphic Stairway. The 50-foot-wide staircase rises up the west face of a pyramid in the very center of the city. More than 2,000 glyphs chronicling the entire history of Copán's rulers are carved into the foot-and-a-half-high risers. It is the longest Mayan inscription

IN THEIR OWN WORDS

All Was Mystery

In 1841, *Incidents of Travels in Central America, Chiapas and Yucatan* became an instant bestseller. Author John Lloyd Stephens recounted his adventures among the Maya ruins, while architect and illustrator Frederick Catherwood (1799–1854) provided intricate drawings of ruined cities. These tales of lost civilizations captured the imaginations of readers all over the world. Here, Stephens describes their first encounter with Copán.

Architecture, sculpture, and painting, all the arts which embellish life, had flourished in this overgrown forest; orators, warriors, and statesmen, beauty, ambition, and glory, had lived and passed away, and none knew that such things had been, or could tell of their past existence. Books, the records of knowledge, are silent on this theme. The city was desolate. No remnant of this race hangs round the ruins, with traditions handed down from father to son, and from generation to generation.

It lay before us like a shattered bark in the midst of the ocean, her masts gone, her name effaced, her crew perished, and none to tell whence she came, to whom she belonged, how long on her voyage, or what caused her destruction; her lost people to be traced only by some fancied resemblance in the construction of the vessel, and, perhaps never to be known at all. The place where we sat, was it a citadel from which an unknown people had sounded the trumpet of war? or a temple for the worship of the God of peace? or did the inhabitants worship the idols made with their own hands, and offer sacrifices on the stones before them? All was mystery, dark, impenetrable mystery, and every circumstance increased it.

(Source: Stephens, John Lloyd. *Incidents of Travel*. "Lost King of the Maya." Available online. URL: http://www.pbs.org/wgbh/nova/maya/travel.html. Accessed September 23, 2008.)

found to date. In fact, it is the longest inscription in all of pre-Columbian America. Life-size statues of Copán's royalty decked out in proud warrior dress defy any city to try to attack.

To try to ensure Copán's return to glory, Smoke Shell married a royal woman from Palenque and produced a male heir, Yax Pac (Yax Pasaj Chan Yoaat, r. 763–810).

In an attempt to stop the decline that was draining Copán of its power, prosperity, and prestige, rulers began awarding more and more power to the elite. After 18 Rabbit's capture, Copán began a new kind of power-sharing among nonroyal elites. A council of elites was formed. A mat house was built in the center of the city, where this council of elites met.

Later rulers passed on more and more power. By the time Yax Pac took the throne, nobles living in compounds scattered throughout

Yax Pac was the last effective king of Copán. He had this bench sculpted to show him with all his royal predecessors. In this detail, two rulers are seated on glyphs.

Copán's territory had taken a large share of the king's central authority. By 810, it was clear the dynasty was headed for ruin. Yax Pac was its last effective king.

THE TERMINAL CLASSIC PERIOD: THE BEGINNING OF THE END

The century that scholars refer to as the Terminal Classic Period (800–900) is marked by decline throughout the southern lowlands and growth elsewhere, particularly in the north. The ups and downs that marked Maya history continued. One decade a city was at its height, the next it was almost abandoned.

Archaeologists believe there were many factors that led to the decline of the cities that had flourished in the Late Classic Period. Robert Sharer writes in *Daily Life in Maya Civilization*, "A combination of overpopulation, over exploitation of an already exhausted environment, destructive warfare, and loss of faith in a political system that could not solve these problems forced people to seek a better life elsewhere."

At the beginning of the Terminal Classic Period, most cities in the southern lowlands were suffering from the effects Sharer mentions. By the end of the era, there was no construction, no new monuments, no strong kings in the former powerhouses of the region—Tikal, Calakmul, Palenque, and Copán.

One key reason people abandoned the southern lowlands was that they no longer believed the gods would assist their ruler in solving their earthly problems. The people wondered, why contribute to expensive, massive building projects when the only outcome was a better life for the elite? The labor force dwindled.

Meanwhile, in the Rest of the World

The first Maya pyramid was built in Uaxactún just before the birth of Jesus Christ. The Classic Era in the Maya world started at about the same time as the fall of the Roman Empire and ended as the Vikings were raiding and looting Western Europe. The Early Classic Period coincided with the Tang dynasty in China. The Late Classic Period took place about the same time as the rise of the Arab civilization in the Near East and the Spanish Inquisition in Europe. The last independent Maya kingdom, Tayasal, fell in 1697. This was the same time that William Penn was establishing a colony in Pennsylvania and Isaac Newton was calculating the speed of sound.

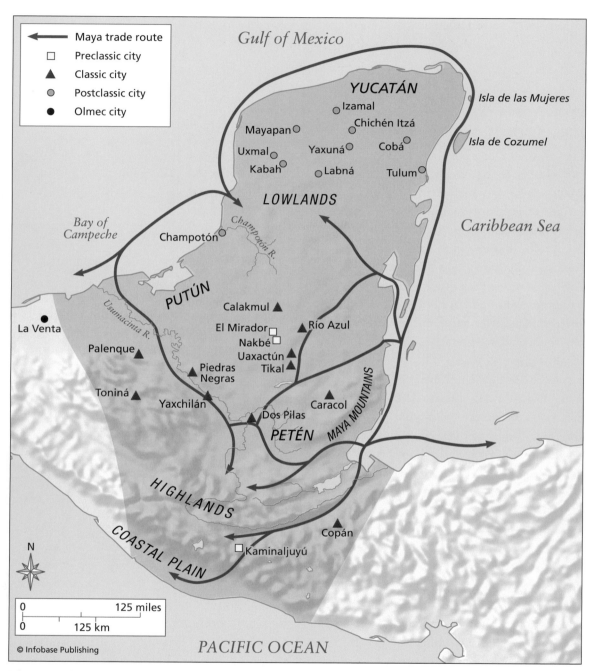

Maya trade route ←

□ Preclassic city

▲ Classic city

○ Postclassic city

● Olmec city

Gulf of Mexico

YUCATÁN

Isla de las Mujeres

○ Izamal

Mayapan ○　○ Chichén Itzá

Isla de Cozumel

Uxmal ○　○ Yaxuná　○ Cobá

Kabah ○　○ Labná　Tulum ○

LOWLANDS

Caribbean Sea

Bay of Campeche

Champotón ○

Champotón R.

PUTÚN

Usumacinta R.

La Venta ●

Calakmul ▲

El Mirador □　○ Río Azul

Nakbé □

Uaxactún ▲

Palenque ▲

Piedras Negras ▲

Tikal ▲

Toniná ▲

Yaxchilán ▲

Caracol ▲

Dos Pilas ▲

PETÉN

MAYA MOUNTAINS

HIGHLANDS

COASTAL PLAIN

Copán ▲

Kaminaljuyú □

N

0 — 125 miles

0 — 125 km

© Infobase Publishing

PACIFIC OCEAN

This map shows the gradual migration of the Maya and the extent of the culture's influence on the Yucatán Peninsula. The map shows the Maya Empire at its height, from the beginning of the Preclassic Era in 1200 B.C.E., to the Classic Era, and finally to the Postclassic Era, which ended with the arrival of the Spanish in the early 16th century.

The elite were no longer satisfied, either. They were still distant seconds to the king. At Copán they had tasted true power and there was no going back. The elite wanted more. The balance of power shifted.

Robert Sharer writes in *Daily Life in Maya Civilization*, "Most Classic-Era portraits show individual rulers bearing all the trappings of supernatural and secular [not sacred] power, alone and aloof, except for downtrodden captives. But in the Late Classic Period the Maya kings began to share center stage with subordinate nobles, who appear on monuments, hold prestigious titles, and live in larger and more elaborate residences. During the Terminal Classic Period the individualized portrait of the ruler is replaced by images of the new leaders in society: the nobility who shared the power within each polity."

Power sharing may have been a factor in the downfall of cities such as Copán. But, according to the archaeologists working there, so was the Maya's serious impact on the environment. Overuse of the land, combined with cutting down forests, flooding, and drought, all played their part in the decline of the Classic Era in the southern lowlands. As the century progressed and the population in the southern lowlands declined, buildings fell into disrepair, fields were left untended, and the great cities of the Classic Era were swallowed by the jungle.

Where did the people go? Some canoed to cities along the coasts. These centers welcomed the newcomers. Others wandered into Yucatán to join existing polities or to settle new lands.

One favorite destination was Cobá in the northeastern part of Yucatán. Another was the Puuc region in the northwest. In the hilly Puuc region, immigrants founded new settlements, including Uxmal, Kabah, Labná, and many others. These inventive pioneers dug cisterns—tanks to collect and store rainwater to be used during the long dry season.

The people of the Puuc region had some kings, but the most common form of rule was by councils of noblemen. Increasing trade also shifted the balance of power. As traders gained more wealth, the economy was no longer controlled almost entirely by the elite. A kind of trader middle class appeared.

Warfare was another factor in the decline. When the new centers grew and began to infringe on one another, the various polities of the Maya found themselves in a battle for dominance. In this, the Maya were no different from the other peoples around them—or from the Europeans who would soon be arriving in the Americas.

CHAPTER 3

THE POSTCLASSIC ERA: RISE OF THE YUCATÁN

THROUGHOUT THE SOUTHERN LOWLANDS, KINGDOMS were dying. The great cities of the Classic Era crumbled. But to the north in the Yucatán Peninsula, and along the coasts, populations were rising. The most significant growth during the Postclassic Era (900–1524) took place in the northern parts of the Yucatán and the southern edges of the highlands.

CHICHÉN ITZÁ IN THE YUCATÁN

One rising star was Chichén Itzá. The Maya people who populated this great Postclassic city had migrated northward from the coastal Putún area. They were warriors and traders—traveling the coast by canoe. The people of the Yucatán called the Putún Maya "Itzá," which means people "who speak our language brokenly."

When the Itzá Maya first boldly marched into the region, they overpowered a kingdom called Izamal that had enormous pyramids. Then they settled into a region that was between small polities in the hills and a large, powerful center called Cobá.

Some time around 850, these immigrants established their capital in the center of the northern lowlands, just south of an area along the coast where they could establish a port. The centralized location of their city enabled the Itzá to control the major trade routes of the Yucatán. Chichén Itzá means "the wells of the Itzá." It refers to the sacred cenotes (natural wells or sinkholes in the limestone) in the city.

OPPOSITE

The Temple of Warriors at Chichén Itzá.

Cenote of Sacrifice

The northern Yucatán has no rivers and few lakes. Therefore, when the Itzá chose a spot for their capital city, they selected a place close to two natural wells called cenotes. These limestone sinkholes gave them access to underground streams and lakes. At Chichén Itzá, the Maya used one of the cenotes for their water supply and the other as a sacrificial well.

The Sacred Cenote at Chichén Itzá is nearly 200 feet across at the top. The vine-covered walls drop 70 feet before reaching the surface of the water. In the center, the water is about 65 feet deep.

In the 16th century, Diego de Landa wrote in *Yucatan Before and After the Conquest*, "Into this well they were and still are accustomed to throw men alive as a sacrifice to the gods in times of drought; they held that they did not die, even though they were not seen again. They also threw in many other offerings of precious stones and things they valued greatly; so if there were gold in this country, this well would have received most of it, so devout were the Indians in this."

The Maya threw many valuable objects, as well as human beings, into the sacred cenote at Chichén Itzá. These were sacrifices to their gods.

Archaeologists studying what is in the bottom of the well have, indeed, found many gold objects. They also found the bones of men, women, and children, as well as objects such as jade and shell ornaments, copper bells, and weapons. Most of the bones were from children who had been offered by Maya priests to the rain gods.

The king of Cobá wanted to show that he was not intimidated by these newcomers. So he built a stone road connecting Cobá to its western ally, Yaxuná. This road staked a defiant claim to all the territory south of Chichén Itzá. The 60-mile causeway consolidated Cobá's territories and, at least for a short time, kept the Itzá from spreading southward. But after years of prolonged battle, Chichén Itzá conquered Yaxuná. Then, as Chichén Itzá grew more powerful from its conquests, one by one its rival kingdoms collapsed. Even Cobá could not avoid the slow decline.

The Itzá practiced a form of government in which power was shared between the king and a ruling council. This system was called *multepal* (*mul* means "group" and *tepal* means "to govern"), or shared rule. The governing council was made up of the heads of elite families. Each person held a particular administrative position in a specific territory. No longer would a single individual have authority over everyone. Now issues were discussed among many people before arriving at a joint decision.

Under this system, the capture and sacrifice of a king could no longer cause the decline of an entire kingdom. That is because there were other leaders who could keep things running smoothly. The shared system of government provided some political stability. However, there were rivalries among the elite families who made up the council, and these rivalries could sometimes cause instability.

The Maya at Chichén Itzá began holding council meetings in a new style of building designed with evenly spaced rows of columns supporting the roof. They built these colonnades alongside their stages where traditional rituals took place. This was a sign that the elite began assuming other privileges that once belonged to the king. No longer were kings the only individuals able to perform religious rituals. Rituals such as the celebration of astronomical cycles were now performed by the nobility rather than the king. Instead of family lines and dynasties, artists decorating buildings depicted the relationships of the nobles to one another. One scene carved into a column shows four nobles performing a death-sacrifice ritual. One carries darts and a severed human head. The others carry the tools for the ritual. Their names are listed on the column. A different mural portrays a throne carved in the shape of a jaguar and nobles seated on jaguar-skin pillows—a luxury that was once reserved only for kings. The throne in the mural is empty. Historians think this might suggest that kingly rule had come to an end.

The change in government also affected how the Maya carried out their warfare. Capturing enemies and sacrificing them was still important. But evidence suggests that prisoners of the Itzá were not humiliated or tortured, as had been the custom during the Classic Era. Carvings can be found at a temple known as the Temple of Warriors that shows richly dressed captives who look very similar to the Itzá themselves. Some cultures believed they could absorb the essence of

The Toltec Empire

The Toltec Empire in Central Mexico arose after the city of Teotihuacan suffered a serious fire in about 750. The religion, architecture, and social structure of the Toltec suggests they were related to the people of Teotihuacan. Toltec, meaning "craftsman," is not a tribal name, but the word used to identify Mexican peoples who carried on the Teotihuacan culture. In fact, historians do not know what the Toltec called themselves. The Toltec and the Maya at Chichén Itzá had such a strong influence on one another that historians call their culture Toltec-Maya.

The heads of two feathered serpents decorate the steep stairs leading to the upper section of the Temple of Warriors at Chichén Itzá.

their enemies through ritual sacrifice. It is possible that the Itzá believed this, too, although a definite answer may never be confirmed. However, the extreme shift in how captives were portrayed implies a significant change in policy.

The inhabitants of Chichén Itzá may have been more open to influence from non-Maya peoples than were the Maya of the Classic Era. The high priest's grave, for example, is built over a cave in a manner that resembles the Temple of the Sun in Teotihuacan, a pre-Aztec society in central Mexico. Both cave openings are meant to suggest entrances to the underworld. Other styles from the peoples of Mexico can be seen elsewhere. For example, the flat-roofed temples with columns carved with feathered serpents are similar to Toltec temples in Central Mexico.

Chichén Itzá was far more outward-looking than earlier Maya kingdoms. The nobility at Chichén Itzá demonstrated their influence by adding to the thriving city's public spaces. They broadcast their successes in politics, commerce, and territorial expansion through buildings and sculptures, which historians can now use to understand the evolution of the Maya culture. In addition, the leaders of the city promoted the exchange of goods and ideas throughout Mesoamerica. By adopting customs from outsiders, expanding trade networks, and welcoming immigrants, Chichén Itzá enlarged its cultural tradition.

THE FALL OF CHICHÉN ITZÁ AND THE RISE OF MAYAPÁN

Construction stopped at Chichén Itzá in 1050. By 1100, the city had lost all prestige and was no longer the dominant power of central

Yucatán. The population fell until only a few stragglers remained. Sculptures at the Temple of Warriors were pushed over. Other temples were looted. Historians are unsure if Chichén Itzá's ruin came about through conquest by other peoples or if the destruction occurred after the downfall.

With Chichén Itzá in ruins, Mayapán became the new dominant force in central Yucatán. Although Mayapán was smaller than Chichén Itzá, the defensive wall that encircled the city provided protection against attacks. Living inside a wall has its disadvantages, though. Instead of houses spread apart, each with its own garden plot, the houses at Mayapán were crammed together inside the enclosed space.

Mayapán owes much of its success to two valuable products: salt and blue pigment. Salt was produced on the north coast of the Yucatán, and rare clay was used to make a pigment known as Maya blue that was used in royal sacred rituals. After about 1375, Mayapán seems to have established a trade in Maya blue with the Aztecs. The Aztecs were a rising power in Central Mexico.

Mayapán's kingship managed to survive for 260 years, until 1441. In that year, the Xiu lords led a revolt against the leading ruling family, the Cocoms. The Xius killed all the Cocom family members except for one son, who was away on a trading mission in the area that is now Honduras. Mayapán was looted, burned, and largely abandoned.

The Yucatán splintered into small polities that historians call petty states. Mayapán's sole royal survivor rallied what was left of his once great kingdom and established a new capital at Sotuta, near the ancient city of Chichén Itzá. But it was too late. The last of the great Maya kingdoms had fallen. Right up until the Spanish conquered the region more than 100 years later, these petty states were at war with one another. Eventually, the invading Spanish took advantage of these rivalries. They used one Maya family to fight against another, and then stepped in after everyone was weakened from warfare.

Maya artists produced some of the finest artworks in Mesoamerica. These included beautiful mosaics, such as this one made from turquoise and shell. It was found at Chichén Itzá.

THE NEW WORLD AND THE OLD WORLD COLLIDE

When historians speak of the Spanish conquest of the Maya, they are referring to the cities and their palaces and plazas, monuments and ball courts—not the Maya people. The Maya people survived and adapted. In the 16th century, three centuries after the fall of Chichén Itzá and nearly a century after Mayapán's downfall, the first known face-to-face encounter between the Maya and the Spanish took place.

In 1511, a Spanish sailing ship ran aground in the shallow water off Jamaica. The ship sank and the 20 or so crew members who did not go down with the ship got into a lifeboat without sails, virtually worthless oars, and no provisions. They drifted on the ocean for 13 days. Nearly half died of hunger before winds and current carried them to the coast of the Yucatán.

Once ashore, the situation worsened. Diego de Landa recounts the horror in *Yucatan Before and After the Conquest,* "These poor fellows fell into the hands of a bad cacique [chief], who sacrificed Valdivia and four others to their idols and served them in a feast to the people. Aguilar and Guerrero and five of six others he saved to fatten."

This is how the Spanish told the story. There is little evidence that the Maya routinely practiced cannibalism (although their neighbors, the Aztecs, did). The Maya did sacrifice people, though, so it is likely that the Spanish captives were going to die.

Two of them, Gerónimo de Aguilar (ca. 1489–1531) and Gonzalo Guerrero (dates unknown), plotted their escape. Just before the festival at which they were to be sacrificed, they broke out of their cage and fled. Once again they were captured, but this time by a chief who was a rival of their original captors. According to Aguilar and Guerrero, he treated them mercifully, although he made them his slaves.

These shipwrecked Spanish brought with them a host of European diseases, including influenza, measles, smallpox, and typhus. These diseases had been present for so long in Europe that many Europeans had been exposed to them and had some immunity against their effects. But the peoples of the New World had never encountered these diseases and had no immunity at all.

The European diseases brought by Aguilar, Guerrero, and others spread throughout all of Mesoamerica. They swept through villages, nearly wiping out entire groups of people. One account recorded by the Maya in Guatemala says, "After our fathers and grandfathers suc-

---

cumbed [died], half of the people ran away from the towns. Dogs and vultures devoured the bodies. The mortality was terrible. . . . That is how we became orphans, oh, my children!" (quoted by William Latham in *Guatemala: Heart of the Mayan World*).

THE FIRST SPANISH IN THE MAYA AREA

Francisco Hernández de Córdoba (d. 1517) led the first extensive Spanish exploration of the Maya area in 1517. Córdoba commanded three ships that sailed out of Cuba. His mission was to sail to the Central American mainland and capture slaves to work in the gold and silver mines of Cuba.

Córdoba first anchored off an island he named Isla de las Mujeres ("isle of women" in Spanish; it is off the coast of Yucatán) after the statues of Maya goddesses he found there. He stole all the gold in the religious shrines, then sailed westward. At each stop, the Spanish were greeted with curiosity by the Maya people. They could not help but touch the Spaniard's beards and pale faces, which were so different from their own smooth, dark skin.

The welcomes ended when Córdoba reached Champoton. (Today, Champoton is a small town on the coast of the Gulf of Mexico, where the Champoton River empties into the gulf.) There the Spanish were greeted with weapons by the warlord Moch-Covoh (dates unknown) and his soldiers.

Córdoba gave the order for his ships to fire their cannons. Despite the fact that the Maya warriors had never before heard the boom of cannons or seen

Switching Sides

After the terrible plague of disease, Aguilar and Guerrero were the only survivors in the village in which they lived. Aguilar struck out in search of other Spaniards, but Guerrero decided to live among the Maya.

He married, had children, and became a military advisor and commander. He taught the Maya what to expect in battles with the Spanish, how to build barricades, and how to conduct effective warfare against their European enemy. In the end, Guerrero led the Maya in battles against the Spanish.

John Henderson wrote in *The World of the Ancient Maya*, "He died in 1536 in Honduras, in command of a flotilla of war canoes, defending the commercial interest of Chetumal against the Spanish. After the battle, his horrified countrymen found him among the slain—hair worn long, body tattooed, nose, lips, and ears pierced for jewels."

smoke and fire spitting from guns, they attacked fiercely. Many of Córdoba's men were fatally wounded. Córdoba himself received 33 wounds.

The Spanish retreated to Cuba. Two weeks later, Córdoba died from his wounds. However, before he died, he told his fellow countrymen dazzling tales about piles of gold to be had in the Yucatán. These tales inspired determined treasure hunters in the years that followed.

CORTÉS SETS SAIL

In 1519, Spanish conquistador Hernán Cortés (1485–1547) set sail from Cuba with 11 ships, 500 men, horses, and provisions. His fleet's first stop was the island of Cozumel (Mayan for "island of the swallows"), off the eastern coast of the Yucatán Peninsula. The local Maya people watched the ships sail in and the soldiers come ashore, and hid in the surrounding woods.

Cortés and his men looted the town, destroyed statues of the local gods, and put up a Christian cross. After searching the woods and rounding up the local people, Cortés found one man who spoke Spanish. The man told Cortés there were "bearded men" who lived six days' journey from Cozumel.

Cortés believed the "bearded men" were stranded Spaniards. He decided to send them a letter by messenger. Diego de Landa reported the contents of the letter in *Yucatan Before and After the Conquest*. Cortés wrote:

Noble Sirs:

I left Cuba with a fleet of 11 ships and 500 Spaniards, and laid up at Cozumel, whence I write this letter. Those of the island have assured me that there are in the country five or six men with beards and resembling us in all things. They are unable to give or tell me other indications, but from these I conjecture and hold certain that you are Spaniards. I and these gentlemen who go with me to settle and discover these lands urge that within six days of receiving this you come to us, without making further delay or excuse. If you shall come we will make due acknowledgment, and reward the good offices which this armada shall receive from you. I send a brigantine that you may come in it, and two boats for safety.

Finding a messenger willing to deliver the letter was difficult. The Maya people did not trust the Europeans. Cortés finally persuaded someone to carry the letter. The messenger wrapped the letter in his long hair and set off.

The meeting time Cortés mentioned in his letter came and went. Cortés assumed the mysterious bearded men had been killed, so he boarded his ship and set sail once again. He did not get far before one of the ships began leaking, and Cortés ordered the fleet back to Cozumel for repairs.

While the ship's hull was being fixed, a man paddling a canoe approached the anchored fleet. His clothes were so tattered that he was nearly naked. On one shoulder he had slung a bow and a quiver (container) of arrows. The canoe paddler was Aguilar, the shipwrecked Spaniard who had escaped the sacrificial ax more than two years before. Aguilar had learned Mayan during his time as a captive, and he became a valued translator for Cortés.

THE SPANISH CONQUEST

For decades, the Spanish made repeated attempts to conquer the Maya. The problem was that Yucatán had no single, large, centralized state that could be taken over. Each local polity had to be dealt with separately. Even when a city had been defeated, its inhabitants were likely to run away rather than stick around to be enslaved by the Spanish.

The Spanish found the Maya jungle to be one of the greatest obstacles. Hacking out roadways proved to be a very difficult task. The unfamiliar tropical rainforest, with its sudden downpours and rapid, choking overgrowth seemed nearly impossible to penetrate.

Perhaps because of these difficulties of moving troops, the central part of the Yucatán continued as it always had for centuries. It was largely unaffected by the Spanish conquest that was toppling empires throughout the rest of Mesoamerica. The highlands, however, were not as fortunate as the lowlands.

In 1521, diplomats from the highlands Maya cities of Utatlán and Iximche met with Cortés and swore to be his allies. However, these highlands Maya later attacked other groups along the south coast who were under the protection of the Spanish. So in December of 1523, Cortés ordered fellow conquistador Pedro de Alvarado (d. 1541) to leave

IN THEIR OWN WORDS

Swept Away by the Rainforest

In a letter sent to King Charles V of Spain, Hernán Cortés described the hardship of marching through the rainforest of the Yucatán in 1524–1525.

After having marched for three days through dense forest along a very narrow track, we reached a great lagoon more then 500 paces wide, and though I searched up and down for a way across I could find none. . . . To turn back . . . meant certain death for all, not only because of the bad roads we would have to travel, and the great rains which had fallen, swelling the rivers so that by now all our bridges would have been swept away . . . but also because we had consumed all our provisions and could find nothing else to eat. . . . I determined, therefore, that as there was no other solution I would build a bridge, and at once set about having some timbers cut. . . . No one believed that such a task could ever be accomplished, and some even whispered that it would be better to

return before everyone was too exhausted and weak with hunger to be able to. . . . When I saw how discouraged they were . . . I told them that . . . I would complete it with the Indians alone. . . . So hard did they work, and so skillfully, that in four days they had finished the bridge. . . . When all the men and horses had finally crossed the lagoon, we came upon a great marsh . . . the most frightful thing the men had ever seen, where the unsaddled horses sank in up to their girths. . . . . But still we determined to attempt it, and by placing bundles of reeds and twigs beneath them to support them and prevent them from sinking, they were somewhat better off. . . . Thus it pleased our Lord that they should all emerge without loss, though so exhausted they could barely stand up.

(Source: Cortés, Hernán. *Letters from Mexico.* Translated and edited by Anthony Pagden. New Haven, Conn.: Yale University Press, 1986.)

Mexico and occupy and conquer the highlands Maya area that is now Guatemala.

By reading Alvarado's messages to Cortés, historians have a picture of what happened. He wrote (quoted in Patricia de Fuentes' *The Conquistadors*), "I sent messengers ahead to inform the people of this land that I was coming to conquer and pacify the provinces that refused to submit to His Majesty's rule." After notifying the Maya, Alvarado assembled his horse and foot soldiers and proceeded to attack one city after another.

The landscape and weather presented Alvarado with many challenges. He wrote, "Because of its size and cities, its conquest requires much time, and inasmuch as the rainy season is in full force I decided not to go on and conquer. . . . [N]o matter what I did, or what efforts I made, I never was able to bring them to His Majesty's service, because all this southern coast that I went over has very dense vegetation and mountain ranges that are close together" (quoted in *The Conquistadors*).

The Spanish invasion of the Maya area was met with strong resistance. Alvarado wrote that upon reaching the top of a long pass, "I saw more than 30,000 men coming toward us . . . and although the horses were tired from the climb we waited for the enemy until their arrows reached us; then we charged. Since they had never seen horses before, they became very frightened and we made good pursuit, dispersing them and killing many" (quoted in *The Conquistadors*).

The Maya tried to trick Alvarado at Utatlán. They lured him and his men into the city, where they hoped to trap and burn the Spanish soldiers. But Alvarado discovered their plot. And after hearing the leaders' confessions, Alvarado wrote, "Therefore upon learning from them of their ill will toward His Majesty's service, I burned them for the sake

This painting from the Maya city of Uxmal shows a Spanish soldier riding a horse. The peoples of Mesoamerica had never before seen horses.

of the peace and welfare of this land and I gave orders that the city was to be burned and razed to its foundation, because it was so strong and menacing that it seemed more like a house of brigands [pirates] than of settlers" (quoted in *The Conquistadors*). In fact, Alvarado was known for his cruelty and extreme measures.

Despite the resistance of the Maya people and the difficulties of the geography, Alvarado managed to found a city that he named Santiago. The city is now Antigua in Guatemala—a central location convenient to many resources. From this base, he went out on successful military conquests.

Cortés did not mention Alvarado in his letters to the king of Spain. Soldiers who conquered lands in the name of the king were well rewarded, and Cortés may have wanted to take the credit for himself. In July of 1524, Alvarado complained about this to Cortés. "Had I gone to Spain, His Majesty would have confirmed the services I have rendered him and would have granted me greater favors . . . for he knows nothing of me, and no one is to blame for this but Your Grace for failing to report to His Majesty how I have served you: for it is you who sent me here. I beg Your Grace to inform His Majesty who I am, how I have served him in these parts, where I am, and what new conquests I have made" (quoted in *The Conquistadors*).

Finally, in 1526 Cortés told the king about Alvarado's role in conquering the Maya. In 1527, Alvarado returned to Spain, where he was awarded the title of governor of Guatemala for his services to king and country. He returned to Guatemala and continued to serve as governor until 1541. At the age of 56, Alvarado was crushed under a falling horse. He died from his injures a few days later.

From Horse to God

In 1522–1525, when Hernán Cortés and his men marched across the southern Maya lowlands, one of their horses injured its foot and could no longer walk. Cortés left the horse in the care of the Maya king of Tayasal. The Maya had never seen a horse before and worshipped it as a god.

They paid tribute with food offerings of turkeys and conducted rituals where a shaman presented the horse with flowers. Unfortunately, this is not what horses eat. It was not long before the horse died.

The Maya carved the horse's image in stone and continued to worship it. When missionaries (people sent to promote their religion in a foreign country) arrived in 1697, they discovered the horse's image had evolved into a god associated with thunder and lightening. The Maya continued to pay tribute with turkeys and flowers.

CONNECTIONS

Keeping the Old Gods

Guatemala and Mexico are still home to millions of Maya who keep up their language, customs, and traditions. Many villages still conduct Maya rituals, although they have evolved into a combination of Christian and ancient Maya beliefs.

In the highlands of western Guatemala, the Maya worship a local god called Maximon. Maximon is part Christian saint, part ancient Maya god, Mam. Mam (meaning "grandfather") was a cigar-smoking god of disaster and earthquakes. He also had power over jaguars.

During Holy Week (the week before Easter), an effigy, or model of Maximon is carried in a procession to a villager's home. The effigy stays in that home for the year. The villagers take turns having the honor of hosting it.

During the year, visitors come to make offerings to the effigy, often in the form of cigars. Maximon's likeness often has a lit cigar poked into the mouth of the carved wooden head. The Maya look to Maximon for marriage counseling, health, and happiness. Maximon is not all good, though. He can be a bully, and those seeking revenge often look to Maximon for help there, too.

THE MAYA CLING TO THEIR HERITAGE

The Spanish made every effort to conquer the Maya people. But groups throughout the highlands continued with their traditions and held onto their languages. Just as the people of the Yucatán had managed to avoid Spanish control, so did some people in isolated areas of the highlands.

In the areas the Spanish did manage to subdue and govern, such as Guatemala, the native culture was nearly wiped out. Diego de Landa described in *Yucatan Before and after the Conquest* the way the Spanish punished rebellious native peoples: "There were some among the Indians who kept stirring them up, and very severe punishments were inflicted in consequence, resulting in the reduction of the population. Unheard of cruelties were inflicted, cutting off their noses, hands, arms and legs, and the breasts of their women; throwing them into deep water with gourds tied to their feet, thrusting the children with spears because they could not go as fast as their mothers. If some of those who had been put in chains fell sick or could not keep up with the rest, they would cut off their heads among the rest rather than stop to unfasten them."

Despite, or perhaps because of, the fear this horrific treatment inspired, the Maya people continued to rebel, revolt, and cling to their own heritage. It would be 173 years, on March 13, 1697, until the Spanish military put down the last uprising and declared the conquest complete. Yet even that was not the end of the Maya culture. Although populations were drastically cut down by war, famine, and disease, the Maya people continue, even today, to hold onto their past.

PART II

SOCIETY AND CULTURE

MAYA SOCIAL STRUCTURE

RELIGION AND RITUAL

EVERYDAY LIFE IN THE MAYA WORLD

CHAPTER 4

MAYA SOCIAL STRUCTURE

THE ANCIENT MAYA WERE UNITED BY A COMMON CULTURE and a shared mythology. But they were never united under one ruler. During their peak, the Maya were divided into at least 60 individual, independent kingdoms that were often in conflict with one another. Large kingdoms were made up of several provinces, or *tzuk*. Many of the *tzuk*, as well as the small towns associated with the capital cities, were ruled by nobles who served the king.

Power in the Maya kingdoms seemed to move across the land-scape. Centers of power popped up into prominence, then fell from power as the next great power appeared. Although the Maya people have survived, their cities did not. Over time, the jungle swallowed them up. Creeping and climbing plants covered over towers and temples, and the walls of pyramids were split by the trunks of trees. Howler monkeys now climb the crumbling temple walls, snakes nest in holes between stones, and jungle vines invade sacred sanctuaries.

But deep within the overgrowth, evidence remains of thriving kingdoms that once bustled with 100,000 people or more. Kingdoms composed of forests and farmlands, villages and towns, all revolved around and swore loyalty to a central capital city.

Maya cities varied in size. Some ceremonial centers were larger than many football fields with structures that soared as high as a 25-story building. The Maya built these great cities using Stone Age technology. They had no cement to make walls or steel to provide rein-forcement or bear loads. There were no metal tools—no metal saws, drills, or carving tools. All their tools were made of stone.

OPPOSITE

This head of a prince is part of a statue that was larger than life-size. It came from the roof of a temple at Copán. These figures represented ancestors, and they were placed at the highest level of the temple.

All Maya cities and towns, large and small, had ceremonial centers. Some ceremonial centers were connected by causeways to the residential areas and the land beyond. Small village centers might have a simple shrine or altar. Large city centers might include pyramid-mountains topped with temples, dozens of administrative and religious buildings, as well as residences for the elite, tombs of ancestors, monuments, ball courts, and open plazas for viewing rituals and selling goods.

The plazas were the heart of the cities. While much of European architecture at that time was used to create lavish indoor spaces, Maya architecture focused on outdoor spaces. Most of their indoor spaces were cramped and dark and only accessible to the gods, the spirits of ancestors, and an elite few. Outdoors, however, they built elaborate stages with courtyards and plazas designed to accommodate huge audiences for rituals, festivals, and processions. Linda Schele and Peter Mathews write in *The Code of Kings*, "Maya architects designed their buildings to encompass motion and performance, so that they operated like stage sets in which drama and ritual unfolded."

A good example of the high value put on outdoor space is a pyramid at Tikal. The pyramid encloses half a million cubic feet but has just three tiny rooms inside. All together, these rooms measure less than 15 feet by 10 feet.

Public buildings were built from stone, covered with plaster, and carved with images that indicated the building's function. For example, a ball court might display players engaged in the ball game, a palace might depict a dynasty, and a temple might be decorated with images of gods or the king dressed as a god.

The images were sometimes carved in stucco (a plaster made by mixing lime, water, and vegetable gum). When the stucco hardened, it was dazzling white and as hard as polished marble. The lime for the plaster was obtained by burning limestone. To achieve the high temperatures needed to burn the limestone, the Maya had to burn a dozen or more full-grown trees. And that produced only a knee-high pile of lime.

Maya builders used stone tools to quarry (dig out) and carve the limestone they used for building. Moving stone from the quarry to the building site was difficult. The Maya had no carts because they had no large working animals to pull them. They also had no cranes or lifting devices—although they did have a basic understanding of how levers and pulleys worked. Everything had to be carried in baskets and slings. Large stones were hauled on top of logs that were used as rollers.

In *Living Architecture: Mayan,* Henri Stierlin describes the materials required to build just one platform: "It is difficult to envisage the work involved in the construction of the esplanade [a long, open area for walking] supporting the Governor's Palace at Uxmal, a level area 600 by 500 feet raised 40 feet off the ground. In all it involves some 12 million cubic feet of materials weighing nearly a million tons." That is for just one platform, and not even the largest one.

Construction required many unskilled laborers for tasks such as hauling building materials and mixing plaster. Many specialists were also needed. Architects understood Maya mythology as well as construction methods so that they could properly line up new buildings with old ones. Buildings were oriented on an east-west or north-south axis, which were considered sacred.

Sculpture decorated the building's stone facades (the sides facing public areas) and wood lintels (the supports across the top of windows and doorways). Artists painted murals and added color to stucco bas-reliefs. Some of these craftsmen became so well known that they were hired to work on buildings in other parts of the Maya area.

Diego de Landa wrote about the extraordinary building talents of the Maya in *Yucatan Before and After the Conquest.* He said of the buildings, "[S]o well built of stone are they, it is a marvel; the buildings themselves, and their number, are the most outstanding thing that has been discovered."

MAYA HOMES

Maya homes were built for sleeping and as shelter against heavy rains and flooding. The average home measured about 10 by 16 feet. Generally, it had only one door, no windows for ventilation, and no chimney for cooking fires. Most daily activities were performed outside.

The Maya people built their homes on top of platforms made of stone and tamped (packed down) earth. The platforms were about two feet high—high enough to keep residents dry during floods—with steps

CONNECTIONS

Maya Homes Then and Now

Maya homes have not changed much in 4,000 years. Modern Maya people in Yucatán call their thatched houses *xanil nah*—Maya for "thatched house." They are built on platforms, with corner posts supporting the roof beams and woven stick walls—just as their ancestors' houses were built. Some also plaster their walls with mud and lime.

Just as their ancestors did thousands of years before, shamans perform dedication rituals to get a home ready to live in. A chicken is usually offered to the earth spirits for their generosity in providing the building materials. A three-stone hearth (fireplace) is placed in the center as a burial marker. Under it, parents bury their infants' umbilical cords. When one Maya asks another where he is from, he will ask, "Where is your umbilicus buried?"

cut into the rise. Posts sunk into the flat top of the earthen platforms held woven branches used for walls. Ancient Maya homebuilders often applied plaster made from earth whitened with lime to the walls. Corner posts were often tree trunks in which a natural fork supported the wooden framework of the roof. The roof was then made waterproof by the combination of a very steep slope and thick layers of palm leaves.

Extended families, with several generations, lived in groups of homes built around a central courtyard. Women planted and tended gardens and fruit trees in plots behind the house. When a family member died, they were often buried under the floor of the house. Sometimes relatives built an altar or shrine over the burial place to honor the ancestor.

PYRAMIDS AND TEMPLES

In the beginning, Maya temples looked a lot like the houses the people lived in. They were small thatched huts perched on top of earthen mounds. But as early as 1500 B.C.E., the platforms for these thatched shrines started to become more elaborate. In areas where stone was plentiful, the Maya stacked flat stones to make the platforms for temples.

As the platforms grew in height, stone stairways were added along the sides. By the Classic Era, in major capitals the platforms supported entire complexes of buildings. Often these decorated platforms would have terraces, like the tiers of a wedding cake—broad, level areas that were ideal for elaborate ceremonies. Imagine watching from the plaza as dancers in elaborate feathered costumes performed on different levels.

The platforms that supported temples surrounded the public plazas. These platforms were laid out in a specific order. The temples atop the platforms were also grouped in sacred arrangements. One of the most ancient arrangements was like the three-stone hearth found in a typical Maya home, with the temples arranged in a triangle. Four-sided groupings also held significance to the Maya people. They believed this shape symbolized creation or the opening to the underworld.

On top of the platforms, the Maya built flat-topped pyramids with square or rectangular bases. They called them *witz*, which means "mountain," because to the ancient Maya these pyramids symbolized mountains. All pyramids were considered sacred. They believed the *witz* (both the real mountains and the pyramids) were living, breathing creatures. In fact, architects sometimes designed the pyramids with eyes, ear ornaments, and wrinkled brows carved in stone.

Many pyramids were giant bases for raising temples toward the sky. Some contained tombs for royal burials. Some functioned as both—temple and tomb. During ceremonies performed for the public below, one or two sacrificial victims were hurled from the tops of the pyramids.

Many pyramids were meant for climbing, and were built to give priests and royalty dramatic entrances. Many early pyramids had stairways on all four sides. Later, in Tikal for example, the pyramids were built with one stairway in the front. Hidden stairways on some pyramids enabled the elite to appear, as if by magic, at the top of the structure or from a secret doorway.

Some Maya stairways displayed scenes of ball games or memorials of warfare carved in hieroglyphs. Details of the events were always carved into the risers, never the treads. These hieroglyphic stairways were sometimes installed to remind the people who was in control. For example, a stairway in Naranjo reminds its residents that they were defeated by Caracol. Some ceremonial stairways were placed to exhibit captives or stage a human sacrifice.

In Copán, the Hieroglyphic Stairway contains the longest known hieroglyphic text in the Maya world. The faces of the 62 steps are each almost 33 feet wide. Together, they are carved with 2,200 individual glyphs. Steep ramps on either side of the stairway are decorated with serpent-head and bird designs.

Watch Your Step

The treads of most Maya stairways (the flat part) were narrower than the risers (the vertical part). This is the opposite of a modern stairway. This design resulted in a steep climb that was typical of Maya construction.

Tulum

Tulum was the largest coastal city in the Maya world. Tulum's largest building is perched on the edge of a 40-foot cliff with dramatic views overlooking the sea. The Maya at Tulum worshipped the Descending God. Over the doorway of the Temple of the Descending God, a winged god descends from the heavens and plunges toward the earth. Tulum was one of the remaining inhabited cities at the time of the Spanish conquest. Its final collapse was due to widespread death from European diseases.

Stone serpents and snarling jaguars guard another impressive stairway in Copán called the Jaguar Stairway. Hieroglyphs on this stairway are associated with the cycle of the planet Venus. At the top of the stairway, the temple entrance is an open serpent mouth with curved fangs and molars in the shape of bird heads.

Temples were built at the top of the tallest flat-topped pyramids. They were sacred places and were open only to royalty and priests. The priests and kings climbed the long stone stairways to care for the gods and the royal ancestors who lived there. The rooms inside most Maya temples, are small, dark, and cramped.

In the beginning, the temples were no more than thatched huts. But once the Maya builders began using stone, temple walls were often made from stone. Roofs, however, remained thatched until the Late Preclassic Period, when corbelled vaulting began. A corbelled vault is similar to an arch, but is shaped like an upside down letter V. The Maya built these vaulted roofs by stacking rows of cut stones on top of facing walls. Each row inched inward until the gap closed enough to bridge the two walls with carved stones called capstones. To support the weight of the roof, the walls had to be thick and relatively close together. This resulted in a narrow but tall structure.

During the Classic Era, builders added roof combs along the peaks of temple roofs. Roof combs were light stonework frames holding stone or stucco decorations. Most were narrower than the building below, and varied in height. Lynn Foster writes in *Handbook to Life in the Ancient Maya World* that roof combs "served as a kind of sculptural billboard that could be seen by the populace from a considerable distance." Temple decorations advertised the temple's purpose. Some temples were royal cemeteries. Their hieroglyphic texts and decorations praised the ruler buried beneath, traced royal dynasties, and publicly proclaimed the divine right of the king to rule. Other temples were places where royalty performed rituals and ceremonies. They graphically pictured the blood rituals performed within or offered praise to certain gods.

THE MAYA ELITE

The Maya had a distinct class system. At the top was the royalty—kings and their families. Below them were the elites or nobles. Then there were farmers and workers of all types—including very skilled workers such as scribes, artisans, and architects. At the very bottom were slaves, who were often captives from the frequent warfare among the Maya.

Most palaces were built in the center of the city next to the largest plaza. Palaces sat atop platforms, just as temples did. But the palace platforms were designed differently. Temple platforms seemed to rise into the clouds, while palace platforms were low and spread out.

In cities that thrived during the Classic Era, there were usually rooms at the front of the palace where a ruler might entertain a visiting noble or meet with his advisors. The palace at Uxmal had four buildings. Inside were strings of small, cell-like rooms, connected like pearls on a necklace. There were 80 in all. The palace in Palenque had indoor plumbing and three toilets. Many palace rooms contained sleeping benches and curtains that could be closed for privacy.

Palaces were compounds for the extended royal family, elite members of the community, and their servants and slaves. It is not certain whether all these residences were used full time or were only occupied during festivals and for special ceremonies.

Naturally, the people who paid for these elaborate homes for their rulers had certain expectations. It was the ruler's responsibility to please the gods through elaborate rituals. The logic was that happy gods send enough rain to grow crops, but not too much to flood

Maya Plazas

Maya plazas often served the same function as modern city streets and parks. They linked building complexes, ceremonial centers, and residential areas. These level, wide-open areas provided space for community activities, such as markets and craft-making. They were also gathering places and viewing areas for religious ceremonies. Sometimes they were made from tamped earth and sometimes from stone or crushed gravel. Plazas at the heart of ceremonial centers were covered with lime plaster, just like the buildings that surrounded them, creating a brilliant sea of pure white.

Most plazas were surrounded on three or four sides by buildings. Often these buildings had broad staircases where spectators may have been able to sit while watching political or religious ceremonies, dances, or ball games.

One plaza in Copán was large enough for 3,000 people. Another contained several carved slab-shaped monuments called *te-tun*, meaning "tree-stone." This plaza symbolized the Earth and the monuments symbolized a tropical forest growing from the Earth.

them. They do not whip up violent storms, earthquakes, or volcanic eruptions. In exchange for the ruler's role as diplomat to the gods, the common people provided labor to build and maintain lavish tombs, monuments, temples, irrigation canals, and other public works.

Homes for the elite were made from stone and had decorative work on the exterior. Most had thatched roofs, although some had stone roofs. They typically had several rooms, often with inside pass-through doors between rooms, passageways, and even staircases. Many also had very small windows. People slept on plastered stone benches built along the walls and carried out many of their daily activities outdoors.

Maya palaces were compounds for all the royal family, plus the elite members of the community. This is the palace at Palenque.

The dedication ceremonies for elite homes were more elaborate than those for common villagers. But they were done for the same purpose—to ask the gods to give the home a soul. Often Maya people of all ranks made offerings to the gods that they placed under the floors of their homes. In stone or clay buckets covered with plates, they placed obsidian blades, jade and shell ornaments, mirrors, finely worked fantastic shapes, bloodletting instruments, honey, and other items they considered to be valuable. These offerings were used to open doorways to the supernatural world and solidify the relationship between the household and the spirit world.

The Merchant Class

One important development in the Maya economy was the emergence of a merchant class (a portion of society made up of people who trade goods). When populations become large enough, not everyone is required to contribute to food production. Some people then become specialists.

In the beginning, the specialists, such as artisans, warriors, and even priests, can only devote part of the year to their specialties. But as the population grows and agricultural methods focus on feeding many, the specialists can work full time, supporting themselves through trade—offering their skills in exchange for food, shelter, and goods.

Soon, merchants are needed to conduct the trade of goods. Merchants also are needed to develop trade routes and serve as middlemen in buying and selling goods over short and long distances.

TRADE IN THE MAYA WORLD

Rulers of the capital cities controlled trade and the distribution of trade goods. Laws dictated who could wear luxury clothing such as jaguar skins, who could consume special drinks such as chocolate, and which artisans could carve stone monuments.

During the Postclassic Era, lively markets held in the great plazas of the capital cities were sponsored by kings. The king took his cut from every exchange—a kind of sales tax to provide income for the kingdom. Some plazas were just marketplaces, with their own officials patrolling the area not only to keep the peace but also to collect the king's share. These plazas were designed with trading in mind. Causeways led to the plazas and comfortable accommodations were available for foreign merchants. Just as people do today, the ancient Maya enjoyed their open-air markets. They were not merely places to shop, but also places to socialize and exchange ideas.

EMPIRES OF THE MAYA

Causeways

Raised brilliant-white causeways connected the center of the capital to different areas. These roads ranged from two and a half to eight feet high and were built by mounding rubble, adding stone edges, and then plastering the surface with white lime plaster. In the northern lowlands, roads were often not plastered but instead topped with crushed white marl (a soft form of limestone) that was wetted and tamped down.

Occasionally, causeways were built to connect sacred sites, such as the causeway that connected the Castillo to the Sacred Well at Chichén Itzá. But most often they were built outward from the capital's center.

Some causeways connected one capital city to another, perhaps connecting allies to one another or a conquering city to its new territories. One of the oldest causeways connects Nakbé to El Mirador. The longest known causeway connects Cobá to Yaxuná. It is more than 60 miles long and nearly 13.5 feet wide.

Traders and travelers would have traveled the causeways by foot, because the Maya had no wheeled carts and no horses or other animals to ride. The height of the causeway allowed for comfortable travel during the rainy season.

Not every buyer could be trusted at the market, for counterfeiting did occur. In some periods, the Maya used cacao beans for currency, and occasionally a merchant was paid with beans that had been hollowed out and refilled with dirt. But for the most part, the Maya were trustworthy. Usury (loaning money and then charging extremely high interest) did not exist.

Not everyone used currency for their purchases. Many bartered (traded goods or services of equal value). A woman might exchange a day of weaving for salted fish. A man might lend a hand building a house in exchange for an obsidian knife.

The Maya traded both raw materials such as obsidian, salt, and feathers, and manufactured goods such as cloth, pottery, and jewelry. Local trade was conducted within the community. Regional trade was conducted within similar environmental areas. Long-distance trade was conducted between Maya regions, such as highland obsidian and jade in exchange for lowland salt and cotton. Eventually, long-distance trade included trading between Maya cities and other Mesoamerican cities.

At first, the main purpose of long-distance trade may have been to increase the power and prestige of the elite. Exotic gifts were exchanged between royal families, and these cemented relationships. Associations with distant and powerful kingdoms increased a king's status. Rare items from far away glorified the rituals performed by priests and royalty. Maya art shows kings sitting on their thrones while representatives from conquered or dependent territories present them with sacks of tribute gifts. Sometimes the tribute was in the form of people offered to perform labor.

Merchants might trade craft items in local markets. In the case of surplus (extra) or exotic goods, they might trade over long distances. Over time, as trade routes developed and merchants found markets for goods, trading expanded to include wares useful to the commoner. With the growth of trade, the wealth (and power) associated with trading also grew.

Trade is vital to a growing economy. In the Maya region, the rise and fall of many of the great centers was due to shifting trade routes. The important cities controlled access to raw materials (such as jade and obsidian) or the easiest routes for carrying materials (such as waterways for canoes). To ensure the safe passage of trade goods, it was important to control the entire length of a trade route. In the Late Classic Period, Tikal and its allies battled Calakmul and its allies for control over the primary trade network of the lowlands.

Chichén Itzá in the Postclassic Era was a key stop on an extensive long-distance trade route that reached well into modern-day Mexico and down to Central America. Long-distance trade provided the opportunity to increase the diversity of raw materials and products, and to be exposed to new ideas and technologies.

Goods were carried by porters over raised roads and trails. The porters carried heavy bundles on their backs with a strap across their forehead that distributed the weight and balanced the load. Merchants sometimes arranged for human caravans (groups of people traveling together, often traders) to transport goods overland, using runners to relay messages along the route. The Maya did not use wheels, so carts were never used to transport goods. But all sizes of canoes were used along coastal and river routes.

WARFARE AMONG THE MAYA

Warfare was a common occurrence in the ancient Maya world. But the purpose of warfare was not always similar to modern conflict. Maya kings regularly set out on royal raids to obtain enemy captives. The captives were used by the winning polities as slave laborers and in ritual sacrifice. Those captives who were not forced to work on construction or in the fields were tortured, sometimes for years, and ultimately sacrificed in public ceremonies. This was particularly true for elite captives, especially kings.

Some of the earliest ceremonial platforms refer to decapitation (cutting off the head) as part of a king's duties. The Maya believed that the victim served as nourishment to the gods, just as blood from bloodletting did. The corpses of those sacrificed were often buried in building ceremonies as a tribute to construction. Or they might be buried with the conquering king when the king died.

Although raiding for captives was one major reason for engaging in warfare, it was not the only reason. Sometimes one polity would engage another in battle for access to trade routes, agricultural land,

IN THEIR OWN WORDS

A Warrior's Gear

This is how Diego de Landa described a Maya warrior's equipment.

They had offensive and defensive arms. The offensive were bows and arrows carried in their quivers, tipped with flints and very sharp fishes' teeth, which they shot with great skill and force. The bows were of a beautiful yellowish wood, marvelously strong and more straight than curved, with cords of their hemp fibers. The length of the bow is always somewhat less than the one who carries it. The arrows are made of reeds that grow in the lagoons, and more than five palms long, in which is fixed a piece of thin wood, very strong, in which again is fastened the flint. They do not know or use poisons, though not from lack of them. . . . For defense they had shields made of split and woven reeds and covered with deer hide. They wore protective jackets of cotton, quilted in double thicknesses, which were very strong. Some of the chiefs and captains wore helmets of wood, but these were not common. With these arms they went to war, adorned with feathers, and with skins of tigers and lions. . . .

(Source: Landa, Diego de, translated by William Gates. *Yucatan Before and After the Conquest.* New York: Dover, 1978.)

or water. As populations expanded, demand for resources increased. A ruler of one polity might invade another, burn down its buildings and drive the people away, removing the source of competition. Or a

This figure shows a Maya warrior wearing all his battle gear.

ruler might wage war for conquest. The victorious leader would then take control of the wealth, resources, and people of the conquered polity. This would enhance the king's prestige.

By the Classic Period full-time, well-trained warriors were a part of Maya society. Their weapons were crafted by attaching stone points to wooden spears or darts. Warriors wore battle jackets and carried shields that rolled up and could be strapped to their back. Helmets often were painted with images of animal protectors. To illustrate to the enemy a warrior's ability, he would often adorn himself with strings of the shrunken heads of previous enemies he had overpowered. Kings fought alongside the warriors. They did not stand in the background merely overseeing battles, but engaged in hand-to-hand combat.

A group image is carved into square columns at the Temple of Warriors in Chichén Itzá. In it, an army of more than 220 men appears to march toward the temple stairway. Most of the men are dressed and armed as warriors. They carry spear throwers, spears, clubs, and other weapons. Linda Schele and David Freidel describe the parade in *A Forest of Kings,* "Some of the warriors in the procession are clearly veterans, proudly displaying their amputated limbs. Each is an individual portrait, differing in details from the others. In addition to the warriors, there are other important people. Some have been identified as sorcerers or priests by the regalia [emblems] they wear and the fact that they are not armed. There is also one intimidating old matriarch striding among all of these men."

Wars were waged during the dry season when farmers were not busy and their fields were at least risk. Most often battles were planned to coincide with the time the planet Venus appeared in the sky as an evening star. This ritual element of warfare was also present in a warrior's preparation for battle. Before fighting a warrior spent days fasting and performing purification rituals to prepare his body for what was considered noble service to his king.

Border skirmishes were so common that by the late Classic Era defensive walls surrounded communities, agricultural fields, and water sources. Most often these defensive walls were low and built with stones, but wooden stockade fences were also built to protect the cities.

THE BALL GAME

The ball game was popular among the Maya and throughout Meso-america. Almost every major city had at least one ball court. Some had many. At Chichén Itzá there were 13 ball courts. This is more than at any other Maya city. Chichén Itzá's Great Ball Court was the largest in all of Mesoamerica.

The paved stone playing field of the Great Ball Court was shaped like a capital letter I, with a long center field and two flaring end zones. Some courts marked the center line right on the playing field and some marked it on the two parallel walls that enclosed the playing area. These walls might be straight or sloped away from the court. At Chichén Itzá the walls were slanted outward. Stone hoops were mounted high on the walls at right angles to the ground.

Many of the walls on ball courts were carved with images of the Maya creation myths. Because the ball game was closely associated with the Maya underworld, the courts were built on low ground, often at the foot of a tall pyramid or platform. On the walls of the Great Ball Court at Chichén Itzá, the carvings show images of two figures nicknamed Captain Sun Disk and Captain Serpent. Each holds an assortment of weapons, because the Maya at Chichén Itzá saw the ball

In the ruins of the ball court at Uxmal, the stone hoop through which the ball was passed is still easy to see.

CONNECTIONS

Play Ball

A rule book for the Maya ball game has never been found, but images of the game carved in stone and painted on pottery and walls survive. These pictures of players frozen in dramatic moves offer a glimpse of the game.

The ball was a bit larger than a basketball. It was heavy because it was made of solid rubber. The stone hoops mounted high on the walls were probably used for scoring. The hoops were only slightly larger than the playing ball. The small size of the hoops and their vertical position made scoring difficult.

As if that were not enough of a challenge, players were not allowed to use their hands. Players wore protective padding on one forearm, one knee, and around their midsection. The Maya passed the ball using the parts of their bodies that were covered in padding.

It also appears that the ball was not allowed to touch the ball court floor, because many images show players sliding under the ball to prevent it from hitting the ground. There were likely regional variations in rules, and no two courts are quite the same (even at the same site).

A game directly descended from the ancient one is still played in parts of northern Mexico. The players can use their forearms but not their hands to hit the ball. The ball is very heavy, so typically, one wants to hit it with the hip. By using the whole body this way, a player can push the ball higher up.

game as ritual warfare. Captain Serpent sits wrapped in the coils of a feathered snake.

The Maya believed that the ball game they played was like a battle, and the game ball was symbolic of a sacrificial head. In fact, the ball court may very well have been a place where people were sacrificed by being decapitated (their head was cut off). Next to the Great Ball Court at Chichén Itzá sits a skull-rack platform for holding severed heads, and some images show the ball game played with heads instead of balls.

A carving at the Chichén Itzá ball court shows two teams of seven players each facing off. One player holds a knife in one hand and a severed head in the other. Opposite him kneels a headless body. From the headless body, instead of blood spurting, snakes stream out of the neck on either side of a tree. This symbolizes the renewal that stems from blood sacrifice. The sacrifice of blood nourished the gods, who in turn provided good fortune and fertility. The ball players and the ball game were symbolic of death and rebirth.

The carving at the Great Ball Court also shows the winning team's captain extending his neck toward the losing team's captain—who cuts off the winner's head. This would seem a poor reward for victory. But the Maya believed this decapitation to be a sacred honor. Someone killed in this way was granted immediate entrance into the otherworld (the place where souls stay after death).

This does not mean every ball game ended with the winning captain being sacrificed. It is possible that the images on the ball court retell a mythical story of sacrifice that was replayed in a more symbolic form as a ball game. However, it seems that in the Classic Era ball games were played by elites, sometimes with captive rulers forced to play on the opposing side. The local elites would typically win the game and then sacrifice the losing lord.

ARTISTS AND ARTISANS

Maya artists produced some of the finest artworks in Mesoamerica. These included exquisite painted pottery, delicate carvings and mosaics (pictures made from bits of colored stones) made from shell and jade, detailed sculptures, beautiful gold objects, and masks and headdresses for ceremonies. Buildings inside and out were covered in brightly painted murals.

The most talented artisans worked in palace workshops making high-quality goods that brought prestige to their owners. Most, if not all, of those artisans were elite themselves.

In the earliest days of the Preclassic Era, cooking pots were made from red clay. Their designs were elegant and simple. By the end of the Preclassic Era, Maya potters were creating works of art. Standing figures of people from all levels of society were punched and pinched into shape, then coated with stucco and painted. Figures ranged from a farmer holding a hoe to a king holding a scepter.

Potters still made pots, of course—shallow rimless bowls, pots with three feet known as tripod pots, and, occasionally, containers with lids that screwed on. Maya potters did not use a potter's wheel, but coiled long ropes of clay into the desired shape and then smoothed the surface with their fingers. After baking the pots to harden them, potters rubbed resin (a sticky gum from tree sap) into the hardened clay for a glossy finish.

Although Maya potters did not use a wheel, that did not mean they were primitive technologically. They mass-produced some ceramics by assembly line. The basic shapes were made in molds and

Nonstick Pans

One remarkable advancement of Maya potters was the nonstick tortilla griddles made in the highlands. Talc, a slippery mineral, was applied to the surface of tortilla griddles. It worked in the same way as modern Teflon.

Working with Jade

The most valuable substance in the Maya world was jade. Considering that jade is harder than steel, it is remarkable that Maya artists were able to work it using nothing stronger than stone tools. The difficulty in working jade, along with the difficulty in finding this rare stone, made it highly valuable.

The initial cuts were made by pulling a cord back and forth, back and forth, across the jade, applying sand and water to increase the abrasion. When the cuts were deep enough from both sides, the tap of a hammer completed the break.

Chert and obsidian blades attached to wooden handles were used for carving. Hollow bird bones made tiny drills. A final polish was achieved by rubbing the jade sculpture with the stone powder leftover from the cutting, drilling, and carving.

Jade was the most valuable substance in the Maya world. These precious objects come from Tikal.

then hand-made decorations were added. Each step of the manufacturing process was handled by a specialist, who passed it along to the next specialist in the assembly line, who performed the next step in the production.

Painters made their brushes from yucca fibers and human or animal hair attached to hollow tubes. They also used sharp points for detailed work. The smooth, hard surface of the inside of a conch shell made the perfect mixing pot for paints. Painters made yellow, blue, and white pigments from clay, black from charcoal, red from iron oxide, and yellow and brown from the mineral limonite. Mixing these raw materials with resin made long-lasting, vivid colors.

The Maya toolbox contained a wide variety of tools. Flakes of obsidian and chert (a hard, dark rock) made sharp cutting and scraping tools, and points for weapons. Bone could be fashioned into needles and fishhooks. Wood carvers whittled bows to shoot arrows, handles for stone axes, and loom tools for weaving. Basalt (a volcanic rock), granite, and other heavy stones were used for the heavier

CONNECTIONS

Cochineal Dye

When the Spaniards arrived in Mesoamerica, they were astounded by the deep red Maya fabrics that did not fade. The dye was better than anything they had seen produced in Europe. The red dye was made from cochineal insects. Cochineal insects attach to the underside of prickly pear cactus pads. The female insect manufactures a deep red pigment and stores it in her tissues.

Cochineal dye became so popular in Europe that, after silver and gold, it was the most valued import. Spain maintained a monopoly on the dye for two centuries by spreading false information about the source of the dye (they said it was from fruit, not insects), by prohibiting the export of live insects, and by denying outside access to production sites.

Cochineal dye was used to color the scarlet coats of the Canadian Mounties, the maroon robes of Roman Catholic Cardinals, and, when the American colonists cried, "The British are coming, the British are coming" it was the cochineal dye that gave the Redcoat uniforms their brilliant color.

Cochineal dye is the only red food coloring currently approved by the U.S. Food and Drug Administration. Some foods that are dyed using female cochineal bug parts are beverages, jam, sausages, and maraschino cherries.

Cracking the Maya Code

Until just a few decades ago, no one could read the Maya accounts that were so carefully carved in stone and painted on surfaces. Then, in 1880, Ernst Förstemann (1822–1906), head of the royal library in Dresden, Germany, took on the task of directing a group of German scholars whose mission was to solve the mystery of the complex Maya calendar.

In 1930, a Russian scholar, Yuri Knorozov (1922–1999), studied Diego de Landa's writings about the Maya in the Yucatán. From Landa's descriptions of the Mayan hieroglyphs, Knorozov realized that the system was a mixture of pictures and sounds and that it followed strict language rules.

Tatiana Proskouriakoff (1909–1985) took the decoding to the next level in 1960 by painstakingly examining Mayan texts at the Maya site Piedras Negras in Guatemala. Then, in 1973, a battalion of linguists (people who study language) from all over the world, led by Yale University anthropologist Floyd Lounsbury (1914–1998), united their efforts at the First Round Table meeting of scholars at the Maya site of Palenque, near the modern city of Chiapas, Mexico.

But the final key, the ability of the glyphs to stand for either words or sounds, was discovered by archaeologist George Stuart's son. As a child, David Stuart had entertained himself while his father worked by copying the glyphs with his crayons. When he was a teen in the 1980s, he recognized how the same symbol or groups of glyphs could have different meanings, and how the reverse was true as well. David Stuart realized that a single glyph could stand for more than one thing.

Through the combined efforts of many scholars, the rich history left behind by ancient Maya scribes is being deciphered bit by bit. Gene and George Stuart write in *Lost Kingdoms of the Maya,* "Thanks to them, we can now speak with easy familiarity of such rulers as the great Shield Jaguar of Yaxchilan, who lived to such a ripe old age, or his son Bird Jaguar, who apparently reveled in his hard-earned title, 'he of 20 captives.'"

tools—chisels, axes, and grinding stones to crush nuts, seeds, and maize. In the palace workshops, many specialized tools were available to the artisans working on the elite residences. They covered the royal walls in artwork such as bas relief and murals.

For large carvings on stone monuments, artists used tools made of obsidian, shell, and bone sharpened and curved for cutting into the surface. The monument stones were quarried, dragged to the site on rollers, then roughed out with stone axes and sanded with stones to create a smooth surface. Artists painted a grid similar to graph paper and sketched a draft of the scene and hieroglyphs before beginning the difficult task of carving.

Simple mats and baskets were woven from vines and palm leaves. Mats were used for dining tables, sleeping, and sitting on dirt floors. They were also placed under bodies buried under the floors of houses. Baskets were used for ritual offerings, carrying things, and storage containers.

Paper was made from the inner layer of bark of the wild fig tree. Maya craftsmen soaked the bark and then boiled it in water with maize, lime, or ash mixed in. After rinsing, a layer was laid lengthwise on top of a wooden board. A second layer was pressed onto the first crosswise and then dried in the sun. Once dry, the paper was smoothed by rubbing it with a stone or beaten to make it thinner. Then it was coated with a thin layer of plaster.

Books, or codices, were made by folding a long strip of paper like an accordion. Strips of paper were also used in blood rituals. Blood-soaked paper was burned in sacrificial bowls, and the smoke became food for the gods.

Natural dyes were manufactured from varied sources. When Brazilwood was chopped finely and mixed with water, it made a red dye. A tiny insect called a cochineal that feeds on prickly pear cactuses also made a red dye. Logwood produced a deep purple dye. Sea snails from the Pacific Ocean also made a purple dye, but it was not as dark.

MAYA WRITING

Did the Maya learn to write from other Mesoamericans or did Maya writing originate in the Maya area? Scholars can not say with any certainty where and when Maya writing began. But this does not mean that writing was imported from elsewhere.

The earliest texts carved in stone appear fully developed in the archaeological record. But early trial and error could have been practiced on less durable materials, such as bark paper. There is a hint that painting may have come before carving in stone. The Mayan word for the verb "to write" comes from the verb "to paint." If the early efforts at writing were painted on surfaces and later washed away, it would explain the lack of physical evidence of the evolution of Mayan writing.

A Little Mayan Grammar

Mayan texts were read from top to bottom and from left to right. To make a word plural, the Maya added the suffix *o'ob* (usually shortened to *ob*). So, for example, more than one *k'atun* were *k'atunob*. There were no gender pronouns such as he or she, him or her, but prefixes were added to some words to distinguish male (*aj*) from female (*ix*).

Mayan glyphs combined pictures and abstract symbols. These are from Copán.

The Mayan writing system developed in phases. At first it was limited to pictures that could easily be read by other Mesoamerican peoples. For example, the image of a person with their forearm pressed across their chest and their fingers reaching toward the opposite shoulder meant friendship.

Next, the Maya incorporated a feature where a picture stood for an idea that sounds like what the picture shows. (An example from modern English might use a picture of an eye to stand for the concept "I.") Eventually, the writing system progressed to the point where some symbols represented sounds that spelled out words, the way an alphabet does. The Maya hieroglyphic system is similar to the Egyptian system in that they both mix pictures with symbols for sounds.

Robert J. Sharer writes in *Daily Life in Maya Civilization*, "Whatever its origin, the knowledge of writing was quickly adapted for political purposes by Maya rulers—especially the Late Preclassic polities in the southern Maya area—and is the hallmark of early civilization. A few glyphs and concepts were borrowed from other writing systems, but the rest was developed by the Maya themselves to create the most complex writing system in the pre-Columbian New World."

Maya kings and queens took full advantage of this new invention by recording their heroic deeds on stone monuments, painted walls, and wooden lintels (horizontal supports over a window or door). If more private forms of memorials were required, scribes (people who copied out documents) wrote or carved on everything from painted pots to bone and jade objects. Often these personal diaries were buried with the owner.

There was a great deal of repetition in Maya inscriptions. Certain words appear again and again, such as accession (attaining rank), bloodletting, and victory in battle. Warfare images appear more often than any other.

But war was not the only record that concerned the ancient Maya. Scribes tracked the movements of stars and visible planets. They recorded seasonal patterns over decades. These accounts led to the invention of an accurate calendar and predictions of eclipses and other astronomical events. In the end, the Maya writing and calendar systems evolved into the most sophisticated systems ever developed in the ancient Americas.

Maya hieroglyphs were probably meant to impress the common people, but it seems likely that very few people could read or write them fluently. The texts carved onto monuments had a "picture-writing" quality to them. This is probably because most people could not read. By using a more picture-like style of writing on public monuments, the scribes created texts that even the illiterate could somewhat understand.

Although the texts were meant for the common people, the scribes themselves were members of the elite. In some cases they were even members of the royal family. Unlike Egyptian scribes, who never signed their work, some Maya scribes signed their names. This identifies them as the first historians of the ancient Maya.

MATHEMATICS

Although the ancient Maya did not use fractions or negative numbers, they are considered one of the most mathematically advanced ancient civilizations. They are the earliest known peoples to understand the complicated concept of zero and have a symbol for it—centuries before

Ancient Observatories

The Maya, like most peoples, observed the movements of the stars and planets. But the Maya took this science to an extraordinary level by building towers in which to make and record their observations. Caracol, the observatory at Chichén Itzá, looks remarkably like a modern observatory with its dome shape and slits of windows for observing the skies.

it was used in Europe. In addition, the Dresden Codex, which was written during the Postclassic Era, includes multiplication tables—proof that by that time the ancient Maya were performing abstract calculations with their numbers.

The number system used today—the decimal system—is based on the number 10. Each "place" increases by the power of 10 as one moves to the left. For example, 467 is equal to $(4 \times 10^2) + (6 \times 10^1) + 7$, with seven in the ones place, six in the tens place, and four in the hundreds place. The ancient Maya number system—the vigesimal system—was based on the number 20. The Maya counting system used the human body and all its digits, fingers and toes. And instead of increasing place values moving from right to left, the Maya stacked their numbers with place values increasing from bottom to top. So 0 to 19 were on the bottom, the next level was 20^1, the next level was 20^2, and so forth. In this system, 467 is equal to $(1 \times 20^2) + (3 \times 20^1) + 7$.

Maya scribes used three symbols to write their numbers. A shell shape equaled zero, a dot equaled one, and a bar equaled five. A Maya scribe would record down 467 with a dot on the third level, three dots on the second level, and a bar and two dots on the bottom.

Maya merchants used mathematics extensively for calculating values of trade goods. For example, a merchant trading cacao beans for jade would have to determine each commodity's worth in order to calculate an equal exchange.

THE MAYA CALENDARS

The Maya were also masters in astronomy. They accurately measured and dated the movement of the Sun, Moon, and planets. Dates were sculpted on temples, carved on monuments, and painted on pottery. This illustrates the importance of timekeeping to the Maya.

Just as the Sun, Moon, and planets have orbits or cycles that repeat, so did Maya calendars. The Maya believed that history repeated itself and that if a certain date brought misfortune, the next time around it would bring misfortune again. Only by identifying days of bad omens could Maya kings, priests, and shamans perform the proper rituals to ward off the evil.

Calendars were also used to predict the future. Feasts, festivals, celebrations, and commemorations took place on lucky days, often timed to the calendar's cycles. In fact, it would be unthinkable to per-

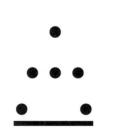

The number 467 written in the vigesimal system used by the Maya.

form a ritual, go to war, or even celebrate a birth, without first consulting the calendar.

The Maya had two main calendars that worked in harmony: a 260-day calendar called the *tzolk'in* and a 365-day calendar called the *haab'*. The *tzolk'in* is the oldest Maya calendar. It was a sacred calendar around which all rituals were planned. It was also the calendar used for prophecy. Dates of the 260-day cycle were recorded by putting the numbers one through 13 in front of the 20 day names, until each of the 20 days had been used 13 times. It would be as if modern dates were written *1 Monday, 2 Tuesday, 3 Wednesday, 4 Thursday,* and so on.

Maya codices were a bit like modern almanacs. They used the *tzolk'in* to predict the fortunes of any given day. Kings used the calendar to guide them in making decisions. For example, a king would want to choose a day of good fortune to wage a battle. (The rising of Venus was a perfect choice.)

In addition to the 260-day calendar, the Maya kept a 365-day cycle calendar called the *haab'* to correspond to the solar year. The *haab'*

The ancient observatory in Chichén Itzá looks remarkably like a modern observatory. The Maya were masters in astronomy.

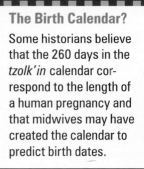

The Birth Calendar?

Some historians believe that the 260 days in the *tzolk'in* calendar correspond to the length of a human pregnancy and that midwives may have created the calendar to predict birth dates.

Thirteen *K'atun* Endings

One major cause for celebration was the end of each *k'atun*, or 7,200-day cycle (about 20 years). There were 13 *k'atuns,* and each had their own specific god and rituals to follow, which varied from place to place. But no place celebrated a *k'atun* ending quite like Tikal. An entire complex of buildings with two pyramids was built just for the celebration.

Some lowlands communities did not want to wait 7,200 days for a *k'atun* celebration, so they had two ceremonies—one at the midpoint and one at the end of the *k'atun*.

A handful of Classic Era sites took it one step further and celebrated *hotuns*, or quarter *k'atuns.* Maya priests performed rituals worshipping the god associated with the *k'atun,* in temples dedicated to that god.

The Maya New Year was also cause for celebration. The New Year celebration began at the end of Wayeb. People came out after five days of hiding from the evil forces and participated in one of four possible ceremonies, depending on which day New Year fell. Each ceremony was associated with a cardinal direction—east, west, north, or south.

contained 18 months, each with 20 days. The *haab'* could be considered the farmer's calendar. Each of the month names has a connection to the earth and growing maize. To make up the last five days of the year, the Maya tacked on a five-day period called Wayeb. Wayeb was a treacherous time where creatures of the underworld traveled through gateways to make trouble among humans in the middleworld.

The 260-day calendar and the 365-day calendar were often used together. Scribes recorded a particular day by its position in the *tzolk'in* calendar, followed by its position in the *haab'* calendar. When the calendars were used together, it created a much larger cycle that repeated after 18,980 days, or 52 years. This 52-year cycle was called a Calendar Round.

Not all Maya calendars were cyclical. The Long Count counts forward (or backward) day by day from a single point the same way the modern calendar works. The Maya were the only pre-Columbian Mesoamericans to use a fixed-point calendar. The starting point of the Long Count was the day the Maya believed their universe was created. This date corresponds to August 11, 3114 B.C.E. on the modern calendar. It is the beginning of the great cycle of 5,128 solar years. The end date of the great cycle—the end of the Long Count—is December 21, 2012. At this point, a new great cycle will begin.

Artists often recorded calendar celebrations on stone monuments. One such monument shows Tikal's king Great Jaguar Paw honoring the end of the 17th *k'atun*. Artists showed him from the waist down, dressed in the same fashion as the kings who came before him. Great Jaguar Paw wears ankle cuffs with the symbol for night on one cuff and day on the other. He stands on the back of a cowering captive and holds the executioner's ax. This captive's death will sanctify (make holy) the 17th *k'atun* cycle ceremony.

CHAPTER 5

RELIGION AND RITUAL

THE YUCATÁN MAYA BELIEVED THE WORLD THEY LIVED in was not the first world to exist. Three other worlds had been created and destroyed by floods before the one they knew. The first world was populated by dwarfs who built the great pyramids and temples. They worked in total darkness, because the Sun had not yet been created. The first sun rays turned the dwarfs to stone. Then the rains came, bringing the first flood.

Although Maya creation myths varied depending on the region and the time period, all the stories shared this concept of multiple creations. Each time, the creator gods tried to make a perfect world. When their attempts proved unsuccessful, they wiped out their mistakes with a flood and began again.

These creation stories were passed on through the generations by being retold again and again. Then, in the 16th century, the highland Maya wrote down their origin myths in a book called *Popol Vuh* (Mayan for "council book" or "book of the community"). It begins before night and day existed, in a shadowy world where, according to the book, "There is not one person, one animal, bird, fish, crab, tree, rock, hollow, canyon, meadow, forest. Only the sky alone is there . . . not a single thing stirs."

POPOL VUH

According to *Popol Vuh*, the creator gods made the first humans from mud. But their design looked clumsy. The book says, "They made a body, but it didn't look good to them. It was just separating, just crumbling, just loosening, just softening, just disintegrating, and just dissolving. Its head wouldn't turn either. Its face was just lopsided. It couldn't look around. It talked at first, but senselessly."

The gods wanted humans to keep track of the calendar and pray to them, and these clumsy humans could not. So they tried again. This time, they breathed life into woodcarvings. The woodcarvings looked human and they multiplied, having sons and daughters. But they were not aware of the creator gods. They did not worship their makers, so the Heart of Sky sent a flood to wipe them out.

A flood was not enough to destroy the next human experiment. According to *Popol Vuh*, "There came the one named Gouger of Faces: he gouged out their eyeballs. There came Sudden Bloodletter: he snapped off their heads. There came Crunching Jaguar: he ate their flesh. There came Tearing Jaguar: he tore them open."

The creator gods turned cooking pots, grinding stones, and tortilla griddles into talking, flying enemies. The grinding stones pulverized human bones. The cooking pots and tortilla griddles sought revenge for being set on the fire and burned the humans. When the humans fled, they found there was nowhere to hide. Their houses collapsed around them, the trees tossed them off, caves slammed shut in their faces. It is believed the descendants of this earlier race are monkeys, which serve

IN THEIR OWN WORDS

Finally, the Best Humans

Popol Vuh describes how humans were created. After several failures, the creator gods decided the best way to make human flesh was from corn.

And here is the beginning of the conception of humans and of the search for the ingredients of the human body. So they spoke, the Bearer, Begetter, the Makers, Modelers named Sovereign Plumed Serpent. . . . "Morning has come for humankind, for the people of the face of the earth," they said. . . . [T]hey went on

thinking in the darkness . . . and here their thoughts came out in clear light. They sought and discovered what was needed for human flesh. . . .

The making, the modeling of our first mother-father, with yellow corn, white corn alone for the flesh, food alone for the human legs and arms. . . . It was the staples alone that made up their flesh.

(Source: Tedlock, Dennis, translator. *Popol Vuh: The Mayan Book of the Dawn of Life.* New York: Simon & Schuster, 1996.)

as a reminder of the consequences that follow when humans fail to worship the gods.

The real stars of *Popol Vuh* were two young gods called the Hero Twins. They were brothers named Hunahpu and Xbalanque. *Popol Vuh* traced their family line to fearsome ancestors such as Blood Gatherer. They were conceived in a very unusual way: A decapitated head turned into a piece of fruit on a tree, then spit in their mother's hand. They were born in the mountains, and their napping place was an anthill.

Many challenges were thrown at the Hero Twins by troublesome characters such as One Monkey and One Artisan. Through these challenges, they learned to be resourceful and clever. But nothing quite compared to their adventures with the lords of Xibalba—the gods of the underworld.

It started with a ball game. Hunahpu and Xbalanque clearly were making too much noise, because suddenly voices came from the Great Abyss (a bottomless pit). "Who's begun a game again up there over our heads? Don't they have any shame, stomping around this way?" The annoyed lords of Xibalba summoned Hunahpu and Xbalanque.

Of course, a summons from the lords of death would not come in an ordinary way. The death lords sent their summons with a nasty, biting insect called a louse. But lice are not known for speed, so to deliver the message more quickly, the louse agreed to be swallowed by a toad. Although a hopping toad is faster than a crawling louse, it is not nearly as fast as a snake. So the toad agreed to be swallowed by a snake. And although snakes can be swift, they can't cover ground as fast as a falcon flies. So the snake agreed to be swallowed by a falcon.

The falcon flew straight to the ball court where the Hero Twins were playing. The falcon vomited the snake. The snake vomited the toad. And the louse, while stuck in the toad's teeth, delivered the death lords' summons.

Hunahpu and Xbalanque climbed down the cliff into the Great Abyss and crossed Pus River and Blood River until they arrived in front of the lords of Xibalba. They greeting each death lord politely. "Morning, One Death. Morning, Scab Stripper. Morning, Demon of Pus. Morning, Bone Scepter. Morning, Bloody Teeth." And so on until they had named them all.

The first night the Hero Twins spent in the Dark House. The lords of Xibalba provided them with a torch and cigars, which the boys were ordered to keep burning all night. But there was a catch: The boys had to return the torch and cigars in the morning unchanged. The boys tricked the lords by attaching bright macaw feathers to the torch so it appeared to be burning. And to make the cigars look as if they were glowing, they fixed fireflies on the ends of the cigars. Witnesses swore they saw the torch and cigars burning all night, and yet the boys returned the items exactly as they were given to them.

The second night, the Hero Twins spent in the Razor House, where moving knives threatened to slice them to shreds. But Hunahpu and Xbalanque outwitted the knives by promising them the flesh of all animals. The knives stopped their motion and put down their points.

The challenges continued. The lords of Xibalba sent the twins to the Cold House, where they tried to freeze them but failed. Next they were sent into the Jaguar House, where pacing, hungry jaguars were ready to attack. But the boys fed the ferocious cats bones. The House of Fire merely toasted the twins but did not burn them.

When each of their attempts to kill the boys failed, The lords of Xibalba wondered, "What sort of people are they? Where did they come from?"

This bas-relief at El Mirador shows the Hero Twins.

Meanwhile, the twins grew weary of the endless challenges. So they disguised themselves as two traveling performers, dressed in rags. They entertained the lords of Xibalba. They swallowed swords, walked on stilts, and danced and sang. And then the clever Hero Twins began to perform miracles. They sacrificed a dog and then brought him back to life.

This stunt pleased the lords of death. "You have yet to kill a person!" they shouted. So the boys killed a human. They held up the bleeding heart. And then they brought the human back to life.

The lords of death were amazed. "Do it to yourselves!" the lords demanded. So Xbalanque sacrificed Hunahpu. His head came off and rolled away. Then Xbalanque brought Hunahpu back to life.

"Do it to us! Sacrifice us!" the lords of death cried. And the Hero Twins did. But they did not bring the lords of death back to life. From then on, Xibalba, the underworld, was only for "the guilty, the violent, the wretched, the afflicted."

The Hero Twins then rose from Xibalba straight into the sky, where one shines as the Sun and the other as the Moon. The gods they had killed followed the Hero Twins into the sky. "And so they came to accompany the two of them, they became the sky's own stars," according to *Popol Vuh*.

THE COSMIC LANDSCAPE

Maya kings, priests, and elites claimed to have special powers. These powers enabled them to mingle with the gods and serve as a bridge between the supernatural world and the human world. Kings were particularly close to the cosmic world. Through trances and other altered states of consciousness, they communicated with gods and dead ancestors.

As agents of the divine, kings were responsible for shaping the world's future. Maya monuments show specific rituals for this. They describe the time, location, and participants.

Images left by the ancient Maya also describe their view of the cosmos. The Maya saw their universe as having three levels. The middleworld, or visible world, was where they lived. The upperworld was the celestial realm of the sky. The world below was the underworld.

The middleworld was depicted as the back of a huge reptile, sometimes a turtle, swimming in the primordial (the first or original) sea. The middleworld was divided into four quadrants (one quarter of the

The Layers of the World

The upperworld consisted of 13 layers, each ruled by one of the 13 gods of the upperworld. The underworld had nine layers. Each layer also had its own god, one of the nine gods of the lower world. The layers were not perceived as separate, but flowed into one another.

Xibalba:
The Place of Fright

The Maya called the underworld Xibalba, meaning "the place of fright." One look at the creatures who occupied Xibalba and it is clear why they called it that. Pock-marked demons with bloated bellies and foul breath wandered the underworld wearing necklaces, bracelets, and anklets made from eyeballs strung together by their optic nerves. Zombies appeared to have little or no flesh at all. Inhabitants of Xibalba were often shown emitting streams of excrement and foul gasses.

The Maya believed kings followed the Hero Twins' journey by descending into Xibalba, matching wits with the demon lords of death, and then rising into the sky to become eternal stars.

Some Maya artists drew Xibalba as being underground. Others drew it underwater, with lily pads flowing on the surface above. There are paintings of kings paddling their canoes and then sinking to enter the watery underworld.

whole)—north, south, east, and west. North was the direction of ancestors and death. Its color was white. South was considered the right hand of the Sun and its color was yellow. East, the direction of the rising Sun, was the most important quadrant. Its color was red. West, the direction of the setting Sun, pointed toward the underworld. Its color was black. Anchoring the center, with green for its color, grew a great ceiba tree. A celestial bird, the principal bird god, perched in the ceiba tree's branches.

The ceiba tree's branches reached up into the upperworld. Its roots stretched down into the underworld, and its trunk occupied the middleworld. It was through this great sacred tree of life that souls of the dead traveled from level to level. It also served as a passageway for the gods to move between worlds.

The orbits of planets, stars, Sun, and Moon were seen as movements of the gods—the celestial wanderers. The Milky Way was the road leading to the world of the gods. Ancestors, spirits, and gods were not confined to the upperworld and the underworld. They also lived among the mortal people in the middleworld. Caves, wells, or any rock formations where water flowed were considered gateways through which the gods traveled. Therefore, caves were ideal locations to conduct rituals and bury the dead.

Maya homes mirrored the cosmic structure. The four poles holding up the roof each aligned with the cardinal directions—north, south, east, and west. The center pole represented the ceiba tree. Hearths were built with three stones arranged in a triangle, copying the Cosmic Hearth—a constellation of three stars that formed a triangle in the night sky. Just as the three stars of the Cosmic Hearth encircled a cloud of interstellar gas and dust, the three stones in the earthly hearth encircled a cloud of smoke.

THE DIVINE GODS

Like many ancient cultures, the Maya practiced polytheism. That is, they worshipped many gods and goddesses. There were gods associated with the natural world—wind gods, rain gods, and hurricane gods. There were gods associated with the heavens—sky gods, moon goddesses, planet and star gods. There were gods associated with agriculture—maize (corn) gods, even chocolate gods. There were gods associated with everyday life—gods and goddesses of commerce, writing, and weaving. And there were dark and dangerous gods associated with the underworld.

Some gods had enormous responsibilities, such as the four Pawahtun whose job was to hold up the four corners of the sky. And some gods were destined to travel long distances, such as the Paddler Gods who paddled their canoe across the Milky Way to the constellation Orion.

The Maya imagined some of their gods as old and some of their gods as young.

The Maya worshipped many gods. When the gods were depicted, the symbols around them explained who they were. This god is shown holding a cornflower.

Some gods took the shape of animals, some were combinations of several animals, some looked human, and others were part human and part animal.

God D: Itzamná

The Maya did not worship any single god as the supreme deity. But some gods were more important than others, depending on the region. In the Yucatán, Itzamná, meaning "reptile house," was considered a chief god. The Maya pictured Itzamná as a wrinkled, toothless, old man with squinty, square eyes, sunken cheeks, and a big nose. Maya legends credited Itzamná with inventing books and writing.

It was not unusual for Maya gods to have several different roles. For example, during certain times of the year Itzamná took on the role of a medicine god and cured the sick. As one of the creator gods, Itzamná played his part in creating the cosmos by placing the third stone in the Cosmic Hearth.

The *itz* in Itzamná referred to a supernatural spirit that the ancient Maya believed was contained in all things in the Maya universe. Robert J. Sharer wrote in *Daily Life in Maya Civilization*, "Everything in the Maya world was imbued [filled with], in different degrees, with an unseen power and sacred quality. Rocks, trees, mountains, sun, moon, stars, and all living creatures—including humans—were animated by this sacred essence." The Mayan word for this animating sacred essence was *k'uh*, meaning "sacredness." The Maya believed that in humans the *k'uh* was in blood. This is one reason why bloodletting was considered a sacred ritual.

God G: K'inich Ahaw

The sun god K'inich Ahaw, meaning "sun-faced lord," began each day as a young man. But as the sun god journeyed across the sky, he aged along with the day and by sunset he turned into a bearded old man.

It was not unusual for gods to have many different looks, depending on their function. During the night the Maya believed that K'inich Ahaw crossed into the underworld after transforming into a fierce jaguar. In the underworld he served as the patron of war. Images of K'inich Ahaw show a ferocious, single-toothed god with catfish whiskers. Sun gods were both worshipped and feared in very dry regions, where droughts and scorching sun could mean starvation.

The Gods, A to Z

Before modern historians were able to read Mayan hieroglyphs, they labeled the gods A, B, C, and so on. Some gods' names are still unknown to historians, so they continue to use the letter names. For example, God L was prince of the underworld and the wealthy god of trade and commerce. He was old, fat, and smoked smelly cigars. He wore a huge brimmed hat on which a screech owl perched. He carried bundles filled with exotic goods and often was shown sitting on a jaguar skin. Sometimes he even had jaguar ears.

CONNECTIONS

The Old Religion

Modern Maya people still worship Chak today. When the dry season comes to an end in the Yucatán, small boys sit under shrines, where they croak like frogs to encourage Chak to make it rain.

Descendants in communities that remained isolated after the Spanish conquered the region, as well as descendants of those who fled deep into the jungle to avoid persecution, continue to practice many of the ancient religious traditions. Potters still make incense burners in the same fashion as their ancestors. Shamans perform many of the ancient rituals in sacred caves and in temple ruins. Offerings such as incense, flowers, and food are burned so that the gods can ingest them through the smoke.

Although they may call it by different names, modern Maya still believe that humans are accompanied through life by a spirit companion whose destiny is interwoven with their own.

God B: Chak

Chak, the god of rain, was often shown holding a lightening bolt, an ax, or a serpent. He was part human, part reptile, and had body scales, large fangs, and snake-like whiskers. Snakes were symbols for lightening. He was often shown painted blue with his hair tied up on top of his head. The Maya believed Chak lived in caves where clouds, thunder, and lightening were formed. When Chak carried an ax through the sky, he struck hard objects, creating thunder.

Chak is one of the oldest Maya gods. Carvings on stelae from 2,200 years ago show Chak performing dual roles. On one stela, Chak is portrayed as the kind rain god bringing rain from the sky and fish from a river. On another, Chak is the aggressive warrior god swinging his ax. Chak appears on the outside wall of the Palace of Masks at Kabah in the Yucatán Peninsula. The palace is believed to have been an administrative building. The rain god must have been very important to the people of this drought-prone Maya region, because 260 identical giant masks of Chak cover the building.

Often Chak was summoned during blood sacrifice. Bloodletting nourished the gods, just as rain nourished the earth. Although Chak was revered, he was also feared. Rain in moderation was necessary for agriculture, but too much rain could ruin crops, and severe storms could be deadly.

God E: Hun Hunahpu

Maize, or corn, was the most important part of the Maya diet. Therefore, Hun Hunahpu (a name associated with the calendar), the maize god, was perhaps the most important of the Maya gods. According to Maya legends, Hun Hunahpu created humans by molding dough made from mixing maize with blood.

To the ancient Maya, Hun Hunahpu symbolized fertility and represented the cycle of life—birth, death, and rebirth. They pictured him as a young, handsome man. His head was shaped like an ear of corn and sprouting maize plants, and his hair was flowing like corn silk.

God K: K'awil

Some gods were particularly important to kings. It was through association with the gods that kings left behind their earthly limitations and gained absolute, divine power. The lightening god, K'awil (meaning "scepter" or "spirit of the scepter"), protector of the royal line, was often carved on royal scepters (symbols of power).

K'awil was portrayed with a snake for one foot and an upturned snout. His forehead was often pierced with a smoking torch or an ax blade. During the accession ritual, in which kings took the throne, they were presented with a K'awil scepter to symbolize their acceptance of power and authority.

In *Popol Vul*, it was K'awil who discovered maize and cocoa by hurling a lightening bolt at a mountain and splitting it in two. Inside two plants grew—maize and cocoa.

God A: Kisim

Kisim, meaning "flatulent one," was the god of death and decay. He lived in the underworld. The ancient Maya sometimes drew Kisim with no flesh, all bones—bare ribs and skull and teeth. Sometimes they drew Kisim with rotten flesh, oozing sores, and a bloated abdomen to suggest a decomposing corpse. Strings of eyeballs formed bracelets and anklets, or wreaths for his head.

The owl often accompanied Kisim. This was a fitting pet, because owls hunt at night and see well in the dark. Maya legends

The Rabbit in the Moon

Today, when we look at the shadows on the face of the Moon we see the face of a man we call the man in the moon. But the Maya saw the figure of a rabbit. In an ancient Maya legend, the first Moon was as bright as the Sun. The gods threw a rabbit at the Moon hoping to dim its light. They saw the outline of that rabbit on the Moon's surface.

describe owls as messengers who fly between the underworld and the middleworld.

Goddess O: Ix Chel

Ix Chel, meaning "she of the rainbow," was a moon goddess. *Chel* is the Mayan word for "rainbow." The Maya feared rainbows. They described the multicolored light as "flatulence of demons." They thought that rainbows came from dried-up wells, which they called "the anus of the underworld."

Rainbows carried disease and were evil omens (signs of the future). They foreshadowed floods, violent weather, and even the end of the universe. Ix Chel in her evil form was shown as old and decrepit with fangs and claws.

Many gods and goddesses took on different appearances depending on which job they were performing. Ix Chel in her kinder form was shown as young and beautiful. She was the goddess of fertility and childbirth, and in this role she often held a rabbit.

DANCE RITUALS

Costumed performers dressed to look like the gods acted out stories from *Popol Vuh* and other myths. The Maya believed that through these dances, mortals were transformed into gods and could then communicate in the supernatural world. Kings, priests, nobles, and warriors participated in ritual dances.

The dancers carried staffs, scepters, rattles, spears, and even live snakes. They wore headdresses adorned with long, colorful feathers that swirled through the air when the dancers spun. Water lilies on some headdresses symbolized the watery deep of the underworld. Kings wore wooden headdresses carved in front with the image of the god associated with the ritual. Some headdresses were made from fabric wound

The Maya enjoyed many festivals throughout the year. Festivals included music and dancing. This plate shows a man playing the trumpet.

Royalty and Ritual

One of the primary responsibilities of kings was to communicate with the gods and ancestors. It was their job to keep the gods happy to ensure order, prosperity, and survival.

Throughout the year, priests, kings, and the elite performed many rituals. Each had a specific purpose. There were rituals for requesting rainfall, for planting maize, for opening a new building, or for destroying an old one. A person might seek courage for battle, cures for disease, or good fortune in trade.

around the dancer's head like a turban. Dancers also wore colorful necklaces strung with beads and shells that clattered with each dance step. All parts of the performer's costume were considered sacred and were stored in holy chambers inside the temples.

Carved on a lintel in Yaxchilán is a picture of King Bird Jaguar IV and his partner performing the Snake Dance. According to the accompanying hieroglyphic text, this took place on October 14, 767. Their elaborate costumes included plumed headdresses of quetzal feathers, beaded and boned breast plates and wristbands, and decorative sandals. Bird Jaguar IV and his partner held snakes.

A scene in bas-relief (sculpture where figures project out from the background) at the Temple of Jaguars in Chichén Itzá shows several individuals performing a dance during Wayeb, the five-day period at the end of the year. Wayeb was an extremely dangerous time of the year. During Wayeb, Xilbalba released demons and evil forces into the middleworld. Disease, death, and chaos spilled out from the underworld. Royalty performed the Wayeb Dance to appeal to the gods for protection from these evil forces.

In the temple relief, the king is shown with flames leaping from his body. This indicates his transformation into a divine presence. The king is accompanied by many warriors. Warriors and women were favorites of the gods because of their courage. Childbirth required as much courage as warfare.

Another purpose of ritual dances was to summon the *wayob,* or the spirit companion. On a vase found in the Petén region from the year 754, six lords from Tikal and Yaxchilán appear transformed into their own *wayob.* Two figures appear caught up in the dance steps, one swings a snake above his head, the other looks as if he is doing a jig in jaguar pants. Two figures are seated—one appears to be cutting off his own head and the other watches the swinging snake dancer. Two figures float above it all holding sacred objects.

FESTIVAL FUN

The Maya enjoyed many festivals during the year. Annual festivals celebrated the change in seasons. There were also festivals to celebrate important events, such as a new king or the opening of an important building. People would come from far away to enjoy these spectacles held in city centers.

Festivals and ceremonies were joyful times for singing and dancing. Priests acted out creation stories from *Popol Vuh* and other ancient myths. Low platforms in the middle of plazas served as stages for the ceremonial dances. Festivities were a blur of color and costume. Dancers wore masks carved to look like gods. Brilliant feathers fluttered and swirled with each movement. Crocodile teeth, jaguar claws, and beads rattled with each step the dancers took.

What festival would be complete without a feast? While musicians, dancers, and jesters (clowns; after the Spanish arrived, the jesters were particularly funny doing impersonations of the Spaniards) entertained the diners, the elite sipped on chocolate drinks. Dishes of roasted fowl and tamales covered the banquet tables. During ceremonial feasts, the Maya drank *balche*, which was made from tree bark, water, and fermented honey.

The Maya enjoyed many family celebrations, as well, from weddings to days that honored their ancestors.

SWEATHOUSES

Maya sweathouses were similar to today's saunas. They were small stone buildings with vaulted ceilings. Steam was created by throwing water on hot stones. The firebox for heating the stones was generally sunk into the floor or built into the wall. The steam rooms had drains

Quetzal Feathers

The long, brilliant-green tail feathers of the quetzal bird from the northern highlands were sacred to the Maya. No ancient Maya feather works have survived, but from Maya art we know that it was a specialized craft.

The highland Maya built aviaries (large enclosures for captive birds) where they bred brightly colored birds for their feathers. But they did not raise quetzal birds in captivity. They believed the sacred quetzal bird could only survive if it was allowed to roam wild in the remote cloud forests of the highlands. Quetzal birds can still be found there today.

Maya Music

At dances and festivals, drummers pounded turtle shells with the flat of their hands or beat on enormous hollow wooden drums using rubber-tipped sticks. Musicians shook maracas strung with feathers. Inside the hollow maracas, seeds or ceramic pellets clattered while the feathers tied to the handles fluttered to the tempo.

Maya wind instruments were made from wood, bones, or gourds. They made simple, one-holed flutes carved from the leg bone of a deer or a piece of wood. More elaborate four-holed flutes might have playful images of gods or dancers molded and attached to the end. For long, mournful tones, musicians blew on conch shells. They also played large, long wooden trumpets and small, handheld ceramic drums and rattles.

Music was not limited to happy occasions. Drummers marched shoulder to shoulder with warriors into battle. Bands of musicians led funeral processions. Special whistles were carved for funerals. The notes were supposed to capture the attention of the gods to let them know a loved one had embarked on their journey through the underworld.

to remove any excess water and benches for the sweatbathers to sit or lie down.

Stone sweathouses were particularly popular in the Late Classic Period. Piedras Negras in the Yucatán had eight sweathouses. This included two in the royal palace and one for the villagers. Among other uses, sweatbaths were used to prepare for performing a sacred ritual and for purification—the steam drove out evil spirits. There are some unusual images found on stelae at Piedras Negras of rulers who seem to emerge from caves. Some historians believe they show kings emerging from sweatbaths after some kind of religious experience.

Sweatbaths were taken for many reasons, including simple hygiene and relaxation. They were also a common part of prenatal care for pregnant women. Sweatbaths were also used for healing. The Maya believed they were a cure-all for everything from aching muscles to poisonous snake bites.

BLOOD SACRIFICE

Bloodletting, or the act of ritually spilling one's own blood, was considered a privilege. To prepare for the ritual, the participant might fast (not eat) for days or avoid forbidden foods, go through cleansing rituals, remain chaste, and even eat hallucinogenic plants to better enter the trance that bridged the barrier between the natural and supernatural worlds. Elite women were shown in Maya religious art piercing their tongues with thorns set into ropes. Elite men were shown sitting cross-legged in what looks like a hypnotic state, preparing to begin the ritual.

The Maya believed that by spilling this most sacred human substance—blood—they could contact the gods and their ancestors. Images of bloodletting rituals appear in Maya bas-reliefs, carvings, murals, and on pottery. In *The Handbook to Life in the Ancient Maya World*, Lynn V. Foster writes, "These bloody acts fulfilled the ancient charter with the gods that obliged humans to nourish the deities with blood drawn from the human body. This obligation had been incurred because the deities, during creation, had willingly spilled their own blood atop maize in order to form human flesh. . . . Maya rulers returned the divine gift of sustenance to the gods."

The rituals probably caused hallucinations. These "visions" were interpreted as crossing over into the supernatural world.

Bloodletting rituals were performed to illustrate the ruler's right to authority and to mark important events, such as taking the throne, births, anniversaries, and special holidays. The tools used to cut and pierce the participants were as sacred to the Maya as the costumes worn during ritual dances. Stingray spines, obsidian blades, and carved bone awls (small pointed tools) were used to draw blood from the body and face. These items were sometimes buried with the individual when he or she died, showing the gods that the person had performed the sacred bloodletting ritual.

Another form of blood offering was the scattering ritual. This is shown in Maya carvings as drops of blood falling from hands. On a lintel found in La Pasadita, Bird Jaguar IV, the king of Yaxchilán, is shown spilling blood from his hands onto a square object near his feet. This object may be an incense burner or altar. The glyph associated with the scattering ritual is a human hand with dots of blood falling from it. The scattering ritual appears to be most often performed to commemorate special dates on the Maya calendar.

HUMAN SACRIFICE

The primary purpose of Maya rituals was to make offerings to the gods to nourish them. Robert J. Sharer writes in *The Ancient Maya*, "Offerings or sacrifices of blood were important because this was seen as a powerful source of *k'uh* [sacred substances]. For the Maya the greatest source of *k'uh* was life itself, and by extension, the ultimate sacrifice was offering the life of a human being to the gods. Thus, the most important and meaningful rituals were sanctified by human sacrifices."

Enemies taken captive in warfare were used for human sacrifice. While the lower-class prisoners were usually used as slave labor, elite

Everyday Religion

Religious ceremonies were part of daily Maya life. People of all levels in society, not just the elite, sought guidance and blessings from the gods. Farmers timed their offerings to the cycle growing maize— planting, sprouting, harvesting. The death of one season's harvest provided the seeds for the rebirth of the next season. Weavers were reminded of the supernatural powers of the cosmos by paintings and carvings on their spinning tools.

prisoners were sacrificed in important rituals such as a new king taking the throne, or dedications of temples or pyramids.

A king would have held the highest value as a sacrificial victim and would have been saved for only the most important ceremonies, such as the recreation of the *Popol Vuh* myth. The glyph that recorded this rare

Lady Xoc's Sacrifice

Carved into Lintel 24 at Yaxchilán is a graphic picture of royal bloodletting. Lady Xoc, the wife of Shield Jaguar, a king of Yaxchilán, is shown pulling a rope studded with thorns through her tongue. This blood sacrifice is thought to take place inside the dark chambers of a temple, because Shield Jaguar stands over her holding a flaming torch.

Lintel 25, the next in the sequence of carvings, shows a bowl filled with bark paper beneath Lady Xoc's tongue. The dripping blood has soaked into the paper. When the paper is set on fire, smoke coils into the shape of a snake known as the Vision Serpent. The open jaws of this two-headed beast become gateways to the supernatural world. From one mouth of the beast, the war god emerges, and from the other a sacred ancestor appears.

Lady Xoc performed this painful ritual to celebrate her husband's rise to the throne and the birth of a royal heir, Bird Jaguar. The war headdresses worn by both figures emerging from the Vision Serpent's mouth suggest that Lady Xoc was also seeking support for her husband's upcoming bat-

Lady Xoc, the wife of Shield Jaguar, pulls a rope studded with thorns through her tongue. Bloodletting was a responsibility of the Maya elite.

tles. The inscriptions indicate that this ceremony took place some time around 724 to 726.

event of kingly sacrifice is known as the *ax glyph* because the ritual climaxed in decapitation. Historians think that decapitating a ruler may have accompanied the finish of a ritual ball game. This was a symbolic representation of the Hero Twins' defeat of the lords of Xibalba, as described in *Popol Vuh.*

Decapitation was not the only method of human sacrifice. The most common method was removing the heart. Robert J. Sharer describes the ritual in *The Ancient Maya:* "The intended victim was stripped, painted blue (the sacrificial color), and adorned with special peaked headdress, then led to the place of sacrifice, usually either the temple courtyard or the summit of a temple platform."

Maya Blue

When archaeologists dug out the sacred cenote at Chichén Itzá in 1904, they discovered a 14-foot layer of blue pigment (coloring). Although most materials would decay under these conditions, the pigment known as Maya blue retained its brilliant color through the centuries. This indestructible pigment stands up to weather, acid, age, and even modern chemical solvents.

Historians believe the process of making the pigment was part of the sacrificial ritual. At the edge of the cenote, ancient chemists heated three healing materials—indigo (a dye), copal incense, and palygorskite (a fine whitish clay)—to create Maya blue. It became food for the rain god, Chak.

The pigment eventually washed off the huge number of offerings thrown into the well. It settled into an incredibly thick layer at the bottom of the cenote.

If the victim had shown courage in battle, the body was cut into pieces and eaten by the warriors and chiefs at the ceremony. The hands and feet were presented to the priests. If the victim was a slave or a prisoner of war, the master or captor kept the bones to wear as evidence of his superior skill.

At Chichén Itzá, sacrificial victims were thrown alive into the sacred cenote. In times of hardship—drought, famine, disease—citizens made offerings to the gods by throwing valuable objects into the well. In 1904, archaeologists dug up the sacred cenote and found gold, masks, pottery bowls, jade beads, carved jade, shells, carved human bones, sacrificial knives, copper bells, ceremonial axes, as well as about 50 human skulls and many other human bones.

Not all human offerings ended in death. Some humans were thrown into the well to speak to the gods whom the Maya believed lived inside the cenote. Children were favored for this task. Priests tossed the children into the cenote at daybreak and pulled them out with ropes at noon to find out what the gods had said would happen in the future.

CHAPTER 6

EVERYDAY LIFE IN THE MAYA WORLD

MAYA DAILY LIFE VARIED ACCORDING TO THE PARTICULAR region a person lived in, the period of history, and the person's status. Which crops to grow was determined by the environment and by what natural resources were available. And as time marched on through the Preclassic, Classic, and Postclassic Eras, daily life was affected by whether the city a person lived in was in a period of growth or a period of decline.

No matter what Maya region or period in history, though, daily living for the elite was very different from the lifestyle of the ordinary people. Three-quarters of the Maya population worked hard to provide food for themselves and the remaining quarter—the rulers, priests, shamans, and full-time specialists such as merchants, painters, potters, and stoneworkers. Despite all these differences, the Maya had more in common with one another than they did with other peoples of Mesoamerica.

MAYA MARRIAGE

Marriages were important to the community. They established economic and social alliances. Marriages were arranged when children were young, sometimes infants. There were only a few rules: The couple could not have the same surname, and someone whose husband or wife had died could not marry into the family of his or her dead spouse.

OPPOSITE
A Maya woman holds her baby in this figure. The Maya liked to have many children. Notice the fashionable, complicated design of her hair.

IN THEIR OWN WORDS

A Typical Town

Much of what is known about the daily lives of the ancient Maya comes from Diego de Landa. His collection of essays about different facets of Maya life were published as *Yucatán Before and After the Conquest*.

Before the Spaniards subdued the country the Indians lived together in well ordered communities; they kept the ground in excellent condition, free from noxious vegetation and planted with fine trees. The habitation was as follows: in the center of the town were the temples, with beautiful plazas, and around the temples stood the houses of the chiefs and the priests and next to those of the leading men. Closest to these came the houses of those who were wealthiest and most esteemed and at the borders of the town were the houses of the common people. The wells, where they were few, were near the houses of the chiefs; their plantations were set out in the trees for making wine, and sown with cotton, pepper, and maize.

(Source: Landa, Diego de, translated by William Gates. *Yucatán Before and After the Conquest.* New York: Dover, 1978.)

Often the bride and groom were from the same town and almost always the same social class.

In general, couples married when they were about 20 years old, except during times of population decline. Then couples married as young as 12 years old.

The marriage ceremony was performed by a priest and usually took place in the bride's home. The priest burned incense as an offering to the gods and gave his blessing for the good fortune of the marriage. A celebratory feast followed.

The newly married couple lived in the wife's family home for the first six or seven years, while the husband worked for the family to pay for his bride. If the husband was not a good worker, the family threw him out. If the marriage was an unhappy one, either partner could declare the marriage over and that was the end of it. Both were free to remarry.

While living with his in-laws, the husband built a house next to the one where his own family lived. After the marriage debt had been paid, the couple lived the rest of their lives in the husband's family complex.

Sons inherited wealth and property from their fathers. Women were able to keep their personal property, but had no right to inherit land. When a family member died, they were usually buried under the floor of the house or in a nearby family plot.

CHILDREN AND THE FAMILY

The Maya loved their children. As soon as a woman married, she began praying and making offerings to the goddess of childbirth, Ix Chel, in hopes of being blessed with many children.

As with all events in the Maya world, a child's fate was determined by the sacred 260-day calendar. Each day of the calendar was associated with a different god. Some were kindly and some were not. If a baby was born on a day considered unlucky, the birth date was quickly changed to a luckier day.

Local priests named Maya babies in a special naming ceremony. The priest consulted the sacred calendar to determine what name best suited the child's temperament and destiny. This was only one of many names given to Maya children. They also had a family name that was a combination of the mother's and father's surnames. For example, a boy whose mother's surname was Chel and whose father's surname was Negri would be named Nachelnegri—son of Chel and Negri.

The Maya celebrated many milestones in their children's lives with rituals followed by feasts. A few months after the naming ceremony, the *hetzmek* ceremony was held—an event still celebrated today. This ceremony marked the time when children were old enough to straddle their mother's hip. For girls the ceremony was performed at three months of age. This symbolized the three-stone hearth that was the center of a female's activity in the Maya world. For boys the ceremony was performed at four months. This was symbolic of the four corners of a maize field, the center of a male's activity.

To prepare for the ceremony, nine objects, one for each level of the upperworld, were chosen and placed on an altar. Each object represented some aspect of the child's future. For example, one of the nine objects for the son of a stonemason might be a small chisel to symbolize the day he learned the craft from his father. During the ceremony, the child's godfather held the child on his hip while he explained the significance of each object, handing them to the child one by one. Then the explanations were repeated by the godmother before handing the child back to the

No School for Most

The majority of the Maya were illiterate. Education was a privilege reserved for the elite. Schools run by priests and nobles were for the children of priests and nobles. Those who showed promise and were well-connected continued their studies by learning sacred skills—astronomy, mythology, and divination—for performing religious rituals.

Boys in school lived in dormitories. They learned ceremonial dances and battle skills for warfare. It is not known if it was common for women to be taught to read and write, but at least some women were literate. Ancient artwork shows women writing.

parents with the ceremonial words "we have made the *hetzmek* for your child."

In *Yucatán Before and After the Conquest,* Diego de Landa says Maya children had a happy childhood. "For the first two years, they grew up marvelously pretty and fat . . . during the whole of their childhood they were jolly and lively." Children were entirely naked and played with one another near their mothers. This continued until the next childhood ritual, held at about four or five years of age.

It was then that children began to dress like their parents. Landa wrote, "It was at this time that a small white bead was threaded into the boys' hair and he began working alongside his father. Girls were given a string to wear around their waist from which hung a red shell to symbolize their purity." However, these objects were still marks of childhood, and were removed when a child became an adult.

The last childhood ritual was celebrated at puberty. It marked the passage into adulthood. Priests consulted the 260-day calendar to determine the best day to hold this annual event for all the children who were to come of age that year. A village elder (an older person of authority) hosted the ceremony by supplying the feast and assisting in the ceremony. After the priest expelled evil spirits, he performed the puberty ritual, called "the descent of the gods," for the assembled adolescents. Following this ritual, girls continued to live at home. But boys moved into a community dormitory until they got married.

LIFE AT HOME

Close family bonds developed from extended families living together in residential compounds. Each house in the group of family homes faced a common courtyard where many of the daily activities were carried out. Families performed daily chores such as caring for the family garden. New generations learned skills such as weaving or making pottery in the courtyard or under covered porches.

Maya women were skilled cooks. They gathered herbs to season their dishes and used chili peppers they grew in their gardens. A favorite meal was maize dough wrapped in cornhusks and steamed with beans—tamales. Maya women mostly cooked outside under thatched roofs that sheltered them from the sun and the rain. They made simple meals with the three staples of all Mesoamerican diets: maize, beans, and squash. The maize was soaked overnight in lime and water, and the kernels softened by morning. The women cooked it to make a curd that they drank hot. They also made tortillas (a flat bread) from ground kernels that only tasted good warm. This kept the Maya women busy cooking tortillas twice a day.

Men and women never ate together. They sat apart on the ground using a mat on which to spread out their dishes. During the growing season, men spent their days working the fields while the women cooked over three-stoned hearths. During the harvest, women and children would sometimes go and live in the fields next to the corn with their husbands. In some communities, the fields were right next to the houses.

When farming demands lessened, the men joined the women under the outdoor awnings, crafting and sharpening their tools, while the women spun thread and wove cloth. The most artistic people in the family might take this time to paint gourds to make attractive serving bowls for food.

Making pottery, both practical and beautiful, was an important skill in the Maya world.

Landa describes the interior of the Maya homes in *Yucatán Before and After the Conquest*. "They then run a wall lengthways of the whole house, leaving certain doorways into the half which they call the back of the house, where they have their beds. The other half they whiten with a very fine whitewash, and the chiefs also have beautiful frescos [a type of wall painting] there. This part serves for the reception and lodging of guests and has no doorway but is open along the whole length of the house. The roof drops very low in the front as protection against sun and rain; also, they say, the better to defend the interior from enemies. . . ."

Kitchen gardens planted alongside each cluster of homes provided the extended family with herbs for seasoning, tomatoes, chili peppers, sweet potatoes, avocadoes, tropical fruits such as papaya and pineapple for cooking, gourds for bowls, and agave plants to make rope. Herbs were not only grown as spices, but also for medicinal purposes. The Maya understood the healing powers of many plants and grew them for home remedies.

CONNECTIONS

Tamales

Tamales are packets of corn dough with a savory or sweet filling. They are wrapped in corn husks or banana or other leaves, then steamed and eaten. They have been a favorite Mesoamerican dish for hundreds of years.

The first tamales were made with ground maize and flavored with oils extracted from avocado and sesame plants. Originally, tamales might be stuffed with beans and chilies. Toasted squash seeds and flowers, meat, fish, and fowl were also used as fillings. Deer meat, especially the heart, was favored for special offerings.

The Maya also produced artistic, elaborate tamales. Some were rolled out, filled, and then rolled up like a jelly roll. When they were cut, the spiral designs were visible. These fancy tamales can be seen in the banquet scenes depicted on Maya vases. The spinach-like herb called *chaya*, still widely used in the Maya regions of Mexico, was one alternative to using corn husks as tamale wrappers.

It is likely that tamales came to the United States by way of the Mississippi Delta in the early 20th century. At the time, workers from Central America traveled through Texas and Arkansas to harvest cotton. They brought their tasty tamale recipes with them.

Today, there are countless regional tamale variations throughout Latin America, and each family has their own recipes. In Guatemala they are a special treat enjoyed at birthday and wedding celebrations, and are especially popular during the Christmas season.

THE IDEAL BEAUTY

The Maya had a very specific idea of what made a person physically beautiful. To achieve that look, shortly after birth, while an infant's head could still be shaped, parents tied two boards to their baby's head. This made the head long and thin. The idea was to mold the children's heads to resemble the shape of an ear of corn. The board positioned in front forced the forehead to slope back, while the board in back forced the back of the head to slope forward.

The Maya also liked the look of slightly crossed eyes. To achieve this, parents tied a soft ball to the baby's bangs so the ball would dangle between the eyes. The baby would watch it, and after a time the eyes remained crossed. The Maya also admired a prominent hooked nose.

As the children grew older, they continued to add the details that made up a classic Maya beauty. They pierced their ears, nose, and lower lip and tattooed their bodies in delicate patterns. The more tattoos the better. Some Maya filed their teeth in patterns and inlaid them with jade or other stones.

Body painting was also popular among the Maya. Warriors painted themselves black and red, circling their eyes and nose with broad rings to make them appear fierce. Women painted their faces and bodies red. Priests painted themselves blue, a color associated with sacrificial rituals. Single men and anyone preparing for a sacred ritual by fasting or cleansing painted their bodies black. Prisoners were painted in black and white stripes, and sacrificial victims were painted blue.

Both sexes wore their hair long. Some men cut the hair on the sides and tops of their heads, leaving a long section in the back. This style accentuated the ear-of-corn shape of the head, with the remaining hair supposedly looking like corn silk. Sometimes men braided the hair and wove feathers and beads into the braid.

Women styled their hair into elaborate headdresses, weaving and braiding it into complicated designs. Women wove turbans into their hair. Men also wore turbans wrapped into the shape of a bowl.

On special occasions, men wore headdresses made from animal skins and heads or carved figures resembling gods, decorated with feathers, beads, and jewels. The wealthier the person, the more valuable the materials.

Facial hair was not fashionable. To discourage hair growth, mothers rubbed their son's face with hot cloths to remove the peach fuzz in hopes of preventing beards and mustaches from growing later on. If that was unsuccessful, they used tweezers to pluck stray facial hairs and to remove eyebrows.

IN THEIR OWN WORDS

Painful Tattoos

Tattoos were an important part of Maya beauty for both men and women. Diego de Landa described the tattooing process in *Yucatán Before and After the Conquest*.

They tattoo their bodies and are accounted valiant and brave in proportion to its amount, for the process is painful. In doing it the craftsman first covers the part he wishes with color, and then delicately pierces the pictures in the skin, so that the blood and color leaves the outlines on the body. This they do a little at a time, on account of the pain and because of the disorders that ensue; for the places fester and form matter. But for all this they ridicule those who are not tattooed.

(Source: Landa, Diego de, translated by William Gates. *Yucatán Before and After the Conquest.* New York: Dover, 1978.)

WHAT THEY WORE

Maya clothing was loose fitting and free flowing. Their fashions were draped rather than tailored. A cloth woven from hemp fiber or cotton tossed over the shoulders served as a cape during the day and a blanket at night. Women knotted cloth at the chest to make a wrap or around the waist to make a skirt. Men used a long narrow strip of cloth as a loincloth, passing it between their legs and wrapping it several times around their waist. Shirts and blouses were often no more than a cloth with a head hole.

In cooler weather, the Maya layered these items—a cape over a wrap for the women, a kilt over the loincloth topped with a cloak for the men. Commoners wore simple and roughly woven clothing. The elite dressed in finely woven fabric, elaborately embroidered and decorated with brilliant feathers, mirrors, and jewels. Royalty draped magnificent capes made of jaguar skin over their shoulders.

The Maya wore sandals made from deerskin and hemp (a plant fiber). The sandals had two thongs. One fit between the big toe and the next toe. The second thong slipped between the four remaining toes, dividing them into pairs. While commoners merely tied their sandals with simple cords made from hemp, the elite decorated their footwear. They attached pieces of jaguar skin, shells, pompoms, carved wooden figures, beads, bones, or teeth.

Both men and women wore jewelry, but the men wore much more jewelry. Nose plugs (ornaments that pierce the nostrils) were a status symbol. The finest designs worn by the elite were made from jade, exotic shells, and semiprecious stones. In the late Postclassic Era, gold and copper became more easily available and were also used. Most men and women wore several lip and nose plugs.

"Worthless" Chocolate

During Christopher Columbus's fourth and final journey to the New World in 1502, he came upon a Maya trading canoe from the Yucatán. When examining the cargo for valuables—looking for gold, most likely—the Spaniards dismissed what they considered to be worthless beans.

Columbus's 13-year-old son, Fernando, noticed that when Columbus's men spilled these "worthless" beans, the Maya scrambled to pick them up. Fernando realized that these beans the Maya called *xocoatl* were valuable to them. But when his father first tried the bitter Maya chocolate drink, he was said to have made a screwed-up, disgusted face and spat it out.

Ear plugs were so heavy that earlobes sagged under their weight and became permanently stretched. Beaded collars and single-strand pendants were also popular. During rituals, nobles, royals, and priests sometimes wore ceremonial belts, bracelets, and anklets made of jade, turquoise, serpentine (a dark green mineral), or shells.

AGRICULTURE

In large community fields, cotton, cacao, maize, squash, and beans were tended by the men. Cotton and cacao were grown for export as well as for local use. Cacao thrived in the hot temperatures, heavy rainfall, and rich soils of the far southern lowlands. Cotton, on the other hand, was ideally suited for the dry Yucatán climate.

Foods that spoiled easily, such as meat and dairy products, could be traded only in nearby markets. Canoe transport only expanded this distance slightly. Maize was stored in community underground cisterns and granaries made of adobe with thatched roofs.

Cacao beans, which are used to make chocolate, were used for currency throughout Mesoamerica during the Postclassic Era. The Maya harvested the beans by plucking the football-shaped pods that grew on the cacao tree's trunk and branches.

Cacao beans were prepared to use as a chocolate drink for special occasions. These beans were dried and roasted and then women ground the beans into a thick paste using the *mano* and *metate.* After seasoning the paste with herbs and spices such as cinnamon, chilies, vanilla, or honey, the women shaped it into tablets that later could be dissolved in hot or cold water.

To create a frothy top on their chocolate drink—which the Maya believed embodied the cacao's spirit and was the best part of the drink—the women either poured from a distance of at least a few feet, or they used wooden whisks that they spun in the liquid by rolling it back and forth between their hands.

Cotton was grown to make clothing. Cotton seeds were removed from the fibers with a wooden stick. Maya women spun the cotton into thread, dyed it, and wove it into cloth that they offered for trade. Talented weavers working for the nobility made heavy brocades and tapestries of complicated designs, sometimes weaving feathers into the patterns. They also wove fabrics so light and airy that they were like modern gauze. These fine fabrics were used for tribute or by royalty.

My Chocolate

A. R. Williams wrote in *Mysteries of the Maya,* "Many vessels created for storing and serving spiced chocolate show scenes of kings and nobles drinking it, as well as the gods. Commoners may also have imbibed during feast days. Some vessels were personalized with glyphs that read, 'This is my chocolate pot.'"

CONNECTIONS

Ancient and Modern Weavers

In the highlands of Chiapas, Mexico, Maya weavers continue to practice the ancient traditions begun by Maya weavers of the Classic Era. Most of the clothing worn by the Maya living in this area has been woven the old way, on a backstrap loom.

According to legend, the goddess of childbirth and medicine, Ix Chel, invented backstrap weaving. This simple loom is made of wood, string, and rope. A loom has a warp (the vertical threads) and a weft (the horizontal threads). One end of the backstrap loom is strapped around the weaver's waist and the other end is tied to a tree. By leaning forward or backward, the weaver controls the tension on the threads.

Before beginning a project, the weaver makes an offering to Ix Chel. It can take three months working six hours a day to make a *huipil* (traditional Maya blouse) in a complex design. The weaving villages of the highlands each have their own style, using ancient symbols woven into the fabric to

Every Maya woman knew how to weave.

tell the story of the cosmos. For example, abstract snake designs are symbolic of the sky. These Maya weavers reject modern synthetic dyes and prefer the vibrant colors found in nature, such as indigo blues and cochineal reds. Little has changed in costume or method in 2,000 years.

The Maya also had other uses for cotton. Warriors wore thickly padded, quilted jackets filled with rock salt—ancient armor. These jackets repelled arrows so effectively that when the Spaniards battled the Maya, they shed their heavy, hot metal armor for the Maya's cotton version.

Another use for cotton fabric was backpacks. Traders were often shown in painted scenes wearing a backpack. Some of these packs were filled with tribute goods to be given as gifts for nobles and royalty along their trade routes. Finely woven cotton was a valued tribute.

The agave plant was also made into cloth, but the resulting fabric was rough and of poor quality. Commoners wore garments made from agave and roughly woven cotton, while the best cotton was reserved for the elite or exported. Agave leaves were scraped with obsidian blades and used to make rope, as well. The strong rope, known as sisal, is still exported today.

One key Maya trading commodity was salt. It was produced in large quantities by boiling salt water until all that remained was the salt residue. The nobility preferred the white salt from the northern Yucatán salt flats. There, salt producers filled shallow pans with seawater and put them out in the sun. When the water evaporated, they collected the salt. In the Classic Era, the salt works along the coast of what is now Belize were kept busy, as well.

One product was so important for trade that the Maya made regular offerings to its god. That product was honey. Bees in the Maya area had no stingers, so the honey was easily collected from their hives. The Maya made artificial hives to attract bees by hollowing out tree trunks and drilling a small entrance for the bees.

By far the most productive farming area was the plains in the southern lowlands. These fertile fields supported bountiful crop production—particularly maize—making the area the "breadbasket" of the Maya. By applying a variety of techniques to make the most of food production, the Maya were able to spread into areas that had been considered unlivable and even support growing populations.

Preparing fields for planting is back-breaking, and the Maya had to do it without the aid of oxen to pull plows or metal to make ax blades. Fields were cleared at the end of the dry season (January through March), when plants were brittle and easy to cut with a stone tool. In April and May, the soil was turned and shaped into long rows with shallow trenches called furrows. When the first rains fell, farmers sowed their fields using a pointed stick to punch holes in the earth and a bag of seed hanging from their shoulder like a woman's handbag.

They planted maize high on the ridge, and beans and squash down in the furrow. After harvesting in August, a second planting followed. Landa described the collective effort that went into planting in *Yucatán Before and After the Conquest*: "The Indians have the excellent custom of helping each other in all their work. At the time of planting, those who have no people of their own to do it join together in bands of 20

Forest Foods

The Maya also gathered food items from the forest. They chose many wild herbs and roots for their medicinal value. The sap from the sapodilla tree made chewing gum, and is still used today to make commercial chewing gum. In the tropical rain forest, orchids were prized for their fragrance and were used to make perfumes and scented oils.

Swidden Farming

In less populated regions, the Maya practiced a farming method called *swidden*. It takes a great deal of land to farm by swidden agriculture. Tracts of land are cleared by slashing and burning the vegetation. A field can be planted for two to five years, but then it can not be used again for five to 15 years while the soil regenerates. This method requires too much land to be practical in densely populated areas.

or more or less, and all labor together to complete the labor of each, all duly measure, and do not stop until all is finished."

Maize was the most important crop the Maya grew. The maize god, Hun Hunahpu, was considered the father of world creation, and everything to do with maize was accompanied by the appropriate rituals to properly honor him. When the fields were first laid, out they were measured and marked with stone boundary markers. Before any corn could be planted, priests had to determine the best day to do so. Prayers, chants, and burning incense blessed the fields.

One might not normally think of tobacco as a food, but the Maya believed it was the perfect food for the gods. They rolled it into cigars or stuffed it into clay pipes. When burned, the gods took in the smoke. Tobacco was also believed to have medicinal value.

WATER MANAGEMENT TECHNIQUES

By the eighth century, there were as many as 10 million Maya living in the lowlands. The farming conditions in the lowlands were challenging. In the highlands, volcanic eruptions enriched the soil naturally by spewing ash. But the thin topsoil of the lowlands was less fertile. Dry seasons and, in Yucatán, the lack of natural water supplies such as rivers and lakes, contributed to the lowland farmer's challenges. And yet the Maya in this region thrived with nothing more advanced than Stone Age technology and without the use of the wheel or beasts of burden.

As early as 700 b.c.e., the Maya built public works projects to manage their water supply. The people at Kaminaljuyú dug an irrigation canal from a lake to nearby fields. At Cerros, drainage ditches circled sacred centers. They functioned as a defensive barrier as well as a water resource.

These massive projects displayed royal power. The projects were often built by volunteers, because they benefited the entire community. Some labor may also have been provided by captives, although historians are not sure about this. More was accomplished through a labor tax, where citizens worked rather than paying money or goods.

In areas where lakes and rivers were scarce, the Maya lined the natural depressions in the limestone, called cenotes, with clay. By sloping the surrounding area so that water ran into the cenote, runoff filled these reservoirs after rainstorms. They also used quarry pits from construction projects for wells. Tikal's extensive man-made water reservoirs held enough water to provide all the water needs of 70,000 people through a 120-day drought.

The Maya often planted water lilies in their reservoirs. The broad leaves spread across the surface of the water and minimized evaporation. Also, water lilies will only grow in fairly clean, fresh water. So if the water lilies died, they knew it was time to find another water supply.

Because of their efficient methods for storing water, drought was less of a problem than floods. Heavy rains in the lowlands washed away the thin topsoil and crushed seedlings. To protect crops from floodwaters, Maya farmers raised their fields to keep them above standing water in the rainy season. They also cut ditches into the fields to direct water into reservoirs for later use and prevent puddling around the plants. By maintaining these ditches—some as wide as canals—the Maya were able to replenish the soil with the silt they removed when digging them.

In flat and drier areas, they made box terraces (walled boxes) into which they could direct and hold water. Along slopes, they cut series of level terraces to protect the soil and young plants.

ANIMALS AND HUNTING

The Maya did not keep herds of sheep or cattle. The dog was their only domesticated animal, although they kept turkeys in pens and tried to entice deer with corn to keep them nearby for easy hunting.

Hunters used different techniques, depending on the prey. To hunt deer and jaguar, they used snares (a rope trap tied like a noose), spears, or bows and arrows. For capturing crocodiles and manatees (a type of freshwater mammal), they used nets. For quail, partridge, and spider and howler monkeys, they used blowguns that fired darts. To catch tapirs and armadillos, they dug dead-fall traps (a trap made by digging a hole and covering it with twigs for camouflage). And for turtles, iguanas, macaws, and quetzals, they set traps.

Merchants traded quetzals for their feathers, and jaguars for their skins, not for food. No Maya would kill the sacred quetzal, because the penalty was death.

This plate shows Maya hunters. The Maya did not keep domesticated animals for meat.

Fisherman weighted their nets with ceramic weights. They used bone hooks until the Postclassic Era, when they began making hooks from copper. They caught spiny lobsters, shrimp, conch, and fish.

Salted fish could be traded over long distances, because once it was prepared it lasted for years. Far from the coast, fish was considered a delicacy and made an excellent tribute to foreign elite. Inland, fisherman caught frogs, mollusks, and snails in the lakes and rivers.

CRIME AND PUNISHMENT

The specific laws of the Maya are not well known. What Mayanists do know is often from the Postclassic Era, or may even have been an invention of the Spanish who wrote about Maya culture. But it is known that the elite and the common people had different laws under Maya society, and different punishments to go with them. These laws were designed to make clear the social differences among different groups of people. For example, there were laws that prohibited commoners from wearing jaguar skins, quetzal feathers, and certain shell jewelry. These exotic treasures were reserved for nobility.

If a nobleman murdered a slave, it was not nearly as serious as if a slave murdered a nobleman. And yet, some punishments seemed to be harsher for the upper class. For example, if a commoner stole something, his punishment was to repay the person he stole from. If he could not afford to do so, he became a slave until the debt was repaid. But if a nobleman stole, his punishment was to have his entire face tattooed. One look and it was clear who could be trusted and who could not.

Punishments differed not only with class, but also with gender. If a woman cheated on her husband, the woman would be publicly disgraced. But a man cheating on his wife would be put to death.

Town officials served as judges for trials. The victim and the accused stated their case before the judge. He managed to remain impartial, despite the fact it was customary to bring him gifts. If the judge found the accused guilty, he would then determine an appropriate punishment.

For violent crimes, the guilty person was stoned to death, shot with arrows, or dismembered (cut into pieces). Murderers might be used in sacrificial rituals or murdered themselves in a reenactment of their original crime.

For arson, rape, and adultery, death was considered the appropriate punishment. Families of the victims had the right to change the sentence by demanding payment for their loss instead of the death sentence. In fact, families of the victims often had power in the sentencing. For example, an unfaithful spouse could be pardoned by the injured spouse.

MAYA MEDICINE

The Maya believed illness occurred when the soul fell into disharmony. Therefore, curing an illness required shamans to return the soul to a harmonious state. Shamans dealt with disease on both a spiritual and a physical level. They made offerings to the gods, performed spells, burned incense, and examined the sacred calendar to remedy the spiritual problem. But they also attacked the physical cause of illness.

Sweatbaths were part of curing rituals. Many herbal remedies were also effective against illness. For example, a forest herb called kanlol is a natural diuretic (it rids the body of excess fluid) that treats high blood pressure, heart failure, kidney and liver problems, and glaucoma. Herbal formulas were used as dewormers. Ointments made from tree barks served as effective mosquito repellents, preventing diseases carried by mosquitoes such as encephalitis (an inflammation of the brain), malaria, dengue fever, and yellow fevers.

But not all of their remedies were such a good idea. Tobacco was thought to cure asthma. And deliberately causing a person to bleed from a diseased area was thought to be a cure for everything. For example, for a headache shamans would bleed the patient from the forehead.

DEATH AND DYING

When a Maya person died, their loved ones cried quietly during

The Ritual of the Bacabs

Today, doctors have many books in which they can look up treatments for illnesses. Maya shamans also had reference books. One that survived into the period of Spanish conquest is *The Ritual of the Bacabs.* Historians gave it that name because of the frequent mention in the text of the Bacabs (Maya gods).

The Ritual of the Bacabs is a collection of chants shamans used to treat illnesses such as fevers, parasites, burns, bites, rashes, and broken bones. To cure a toothache, *The Ritual of the Bacabs* advises the shaman to repeat, "I stand ready to take his fire. I roast him in the heart of food, in the tooth of the green wooden man, the green/stone man. Red is my breath, white is my breath, black is my breath, yellow is my breath."

This beautiful mask was laid over the face of a dead nobleman in Tikal so he could wear it during his journey through the underworld.

the day, but after dark grievers were loud and mournful. For days, they carried on their mourning, fasting for the deceased. They filled the mouth of the dead with maize and a drink called *koyem* so the dead person would not be hungry on their journey to the underworld. Some added jade beads so the dead would have money, too.

After wrapping the body, the Maya usually buried it under the floor or behind the house to keep their ancestor nearby. Sometimes, mourners threw clay or wood figures into the grave that indicated the dead person's occupation. In a priest's grave, mourners threw in some

EPILOGUE

IMAGINE DISCOVERING AN ENTIRE CIVILIZATION ON MARS. People today think Earth is the only populated planet in our solar system. It would be astounding if one day, while exploring Mars, great cities were found that were populated by thousands of people with their own sophisticated systems.

It must have been like that for the European explorers when they first encountered the peoples of the Americas. They were astonished when they discovered Earth was home to great civilizations other than their own. What a wonder it must have been to hack through thick jungle vegetation and then suddenly step into the open and see soaring temples and pyramids and palaces. What would they have felt as they walked through bustling markets among people whose appearance and language was so foreign that it seemed to be from another world?

FIRST CONTACT

The first known contact between the Maya and the Europeans was in 1502, during Christopher Columbus's fourth and final voyage to the Americas. He happened upon a seagoing trading canoe off the Maya coastline.

Columbus's 13-year-old son, Fernando (1488–1519), wrote that the Maya "resembled those of the other islands, but had narrower foreheads" (quoted in *The Fourth Voyage of Christopher Columbus*). Fernando also described their canoe: "[L]ong as a galley and eight feet wide, made of a single tree trunk like the other Indian canoes; it was freighted with merchandise from the western regions around New Spain. Amidships it had a palm-leaf awning like that on Venetian gondolas; this gave complete protections against the rain and waves. Underneath were women and children, and all the baggage and merchandise. There were 25 paddlers aboard, but they offered no resistance when our boats drew up to them."

THE SPANISH INVASION

The first European attack against the Maya did not come in the form of armies of conquistadors (the Spanish word for "conquerors"). Rather, it came in the form of disease. By 1516, the Maya of the Yucatán had been devastated by what was probably smallpox. The Maya had never been exposed to smallpox before the arrival of the Spaniards, and they had no immunity.

Although there were many small battles between the Maya and the Spanish, the first massive military attack launched against the Maya was led by Hernán Cortés. In 1519, 500 men aboard 11 ships anchored off Cozumel Island. They destroyed the images of the gods in Maya temples and replaced them with Christian crosses. But the lure of gold drew Cortés away, and he sailed on to conquer the Aztecs.

Six years later, in 1525, Cortés returned to the Maya area. This time it was to confront one of his own officers, a traitorous captain who had betrayed Cortés and Spain by claiming territory for himself.

Cortés returned by land. His expedition marked the first time Europeans crossed the central and southern Maya lowlands. Robert J. Sharer described the march in *The Ancient Maya*:

IN THEIR OWN WORDS

Devastating Disease

The Spanish brought many European diseases to the Americas. These diseases may have killed more Native peoples than the number who died in military conflicts with the Europeans. Diego de Landa described the suffering of an outbreak of smallpox in *Yucatan Before and After the Conquest*:

> [W]ith great pustules that rotted the body, fetid in odor, and so that the members fell in pieces within four or five days.

And the Maya themselves record in *The Book of Chilam Balam of Chumayel*:

> Eleven Ajaw was when the mighty men arrived from the east. They were the ones who first brought the disease here to our land, the land of us who are Maya, in the year 1513.

(Source: Landa, Diego de, William Gates, translator. *Yucatan Before and After the Conquest.* New York: Dover, 1978; and Roys, Ralph L., translator. *The Book of Chilam Balam of Chumayel*. Washington, D.C.: Carnegie Institution, 1933.)

"The undertaking proved to be one of the most formidable sustained efforts in military history. Cortés was accompanied by about 140 Spanish soldiers, 93 of them mounted [on horseback], and by more than 3,000 warriors from Mexico, with 150 horses, a herd of pigs, artillery, munitions, and supplies." Sharer marveled at Cortés's sheer determination. "To transport such a large body of men across this wilderness would tax the strength and endurance of a well-organized modern army."

CONQUEST AND COLONIZATION

The conquest and colonization of the Maya occurred 1,000 years after the peak of Maya civilization. The Spanish had a huge advantage in how their military was equipped. They traveled on horseback and were armed with guns. The Maya had no beasts of burden to carry them and were armed with what amounted to pointed sticks against the Spanish guns. But despite this, the Spanish did not easily conquer the Maya. It took nearly 200 years to completely subdue them.

Much of the Maya area was colonized and many of the Maya people were converted to Christianity by the Spaniards by the middle of the 16th century. But it would be another century and a half before the peoples of Itzá in the Petén fell to Spanish rule.

In the end, it was the Maya themselves who provided the means for their downfall. Just as they had throughout their history, Maya capitals fought against their neighboring Maya capitals. By forming alliances with the Spanish against their Maya enemies, they gained some short-term victories against their neighbors. But their satisfaction was short-lived. The Spaniards used Maya allies to help them conquer a town and then conquered the Maya who had helped them.

The Spanish conquest, conversion, and colonization of the Maya was so cruel and brutal that scholars call it one of the most catastrophic events in human history. People were slaughtered in savage ways, and the Maya culture and religion were nearly destroyed.

When the Spanish were finished, the Maya population had been reduced by 90 percent and their religion and culture were maintained only in secret. Robert J. Sharer wrote in *The Ancient Maya* that the conquest "succeeded in destroying the last remnants of Maya independence. . . . The subjugation of the Maya also marked the beginning of a long period of European suppression that has shaped much of the world of the modern Maya people."

MEXICO EMERGES

The Mexican people rebelled against their Spanish rulers in 1810. After a long war, they won their independence in 1821. The new nation of Mexico encompassed the Yucatán and the Maya who lived there.

Although the Maya were now technically a free people within a new nation, the majority had no way to support themselves other than working on the farms owned by wealthy landowners. These landowners were descendants of the original Spanish conquerors. Their estates were called *haciendas,* and the Maya who worked on them were no better off than slaves.

The Spanish landowners took advantage of the Maya's situation and controlled them by keeping the Maya in financial debt. They were never paid enough wages to work off their debt, and so they were forced to keep working on the *haciendas.* Life was not much better for the small communities of Maya throughout Mexico who struggled to maintain independence from the *haciendas.* They lived in extreme poverty.

The 1840s were a time of unrest among the Mexican population. Poverty and the unfair social hierarchy fueled many rebellions. The Mexican government needed soldiers to keep the peace, so they promised the Maya people that if they served in the Mexican military, they would be given land with tax rates that would enable them to break free of their debts to the *haciendas.* But by 1847 it became clear that the government did not intend to keep its promises.

THE WAR OF THE CASTES

Since the Spanish conquest, Mesoamerica had been under a caste system (a rigid ordering of society by social groups), with the Spaniards and their descendants at the top and the native Maya at the bottom. On July 30, 1847, after three centuries of abuse at the hands of Europeans and their descendants, the Maya exploded in a violent revolt. Maya soldiers in the Yucatán massacred men, women, and children. Even infants were not safe from their rage. Armed by the British from what is today Belize, the Maya went on a rampage, looting and burning *haciendas* and villages.

In an effort to put down the rebellion, Mexican authorities drafted all men from age 16 to 60 into the army. Both sides committed cruel and brutal acts. The ethnic Spanish in Yucatán were driven from their *haciendas* by 12,000 to 15,000 Maya soldiers. The Maya controlled the roadways of the region, trapping the Spanish in the city of Mérida.

Inside the walls of the city, the ethnic Spanish prepared an escape to the coast and the port of Sisal, where Mexican ships waited to rescue them. But when it came time to print and distribute the plans for evacuation, there was not enough paper in the town. Rumors began to circulate that the Maya were gathering for a final attack. No one would be spared. For two days, the terrified Spanish waited. Finally, they sent someone beyond the walls to evaluate the situation. The Maya were gone.

Winged ants had come in swarms, signaling the arrival of the first rains. The Maya had rolled up their sleeping mats, packed their travel bags, and gone home. It was time to plant the corn.

THE PROPHECY OF THE TALKING CROSS

In 1850, the largest Maya community that was independent of the *haciendas* was the village of Chan Santa Cruz. The border of the village stretched from just north of present-day Tulum all the way to the Belize border. Carved into a mahogany tree growing in Chan Santa Cruz, a mysterious cross miraculously appeared. The cross spoke to the Maya chiefs. This miraculous Talking Cross predicted a holy war between the native Maya and those of Spanish descent.

The Maya people believed God spoke to them through this cross— and the chiefs interpreted what the cross said. It told them to continue their fight against the enemies of Maya independence. It also told them they must be patient, because the war would be long. It told them how to organize to become more effective warriors. It told them it would protect them against the white men's bullets.

The appearance of the cross made Chan Santa Cruz a center of Maya resistance. The cross gave religious significance to the rebellion. People who believed in the prophesy of the cross called themselves Cruzob or "people of the cross."

In 1851, the church where the cross was kept was raided by the Mexican authorities and they took the cross. Soon after, three crosses miraculously appeared in its place, all with the power to speak, just as the Talking Cross had. The Maya believed these crosses were daughters of the original cross. Their purpose was to continue guiding the faithful.

For more than 50 years, the Maya in Yucatán continued to battle against the Mexican authorities. Twice the Mexican army fought their way to the very doorstep of Chan Santa Cruz and twice the Maya pushed them back. But at the close of the 19th century, the United Kingdom

CONNECTIONS

Monkey Business Theater

The acting company *Teatro Lo'il Maxil* (the monkey business theater) was formed in Mexico in 1985 with the help of some New York stage directors. The group writes and performs plays in southern Mexico, throughout Central America, and for migrant workers in the United States.

Their plays are based on ancient Maya mythology, history, and folk tales. One popular play is *Who Believes in Spooks?* It is about an evil cannibal who roams the countryside looking for women and children to lure into his cave. When the wicked cannibal comes across workmen at temple or pyramid construction sites, he murders them and seals them in the wet cement.

Jaguar Dynasty begins with the reign of Shield Jaguar and Lady Sharká (Lady Xoc), rulers of the powerful city-state of Yaxchilàn. It follows the centuries of bitter warfare that came after their reign, and the final conquest of the Maya by the Spaniards.

These dramatic productions preserve Maya culture and history.

signed a treaty with Mexico and no longer could trade or provide Chan Santa Cruz with arms and gunpowder. Without these crucial supplies, Chan Santa Cruz fell to the Mexican government forces in 1901. The War of the Castes had cost the Maya dearly. More than 50,000 Maya lost their lives in the rebellion.

MODERN MEXICO

In 1915, the Mexican government removed its military forces from Chan Santa Cruz, returning local control to the Maya. Small villages once again cropped up in the region. Most were based on a version of Christianity that centered around the Talking Cross. The Talking Cross religion provided a link for the Maya between their ancient traditions and modern Mexican culture.

Mexico's Yucatán enjoyed an economic boom at the end of the 19th century, thanks to a local crop that was much in demand—henequen. Henequen is a fibrous plant from which twine is made. It was in such demand in the United States that Yucatán farmers called it green gold.

But prices dropped drastically in 1930, probably as the result of a serious economic depression in the United States. Yucatán went from being Mexico's wealthiest region to its poorest. Maya workers could not find jobs. Crime rose as quickly as the poverty levels. Today, the people of Yucatán look to tourism as a way of building jobs and opportunities.

MODERN GUATEMALA

Half of the nearly 20 million people in Guatemala are Maya. Unlike Mexico, where the Maya won equal rights under the law, in Guatemala the Maya still suffer from discrimination. Native Maya are considered inferior to those who are of Spanish descent. Maya farmers have been forced off their land and into mountain areas,

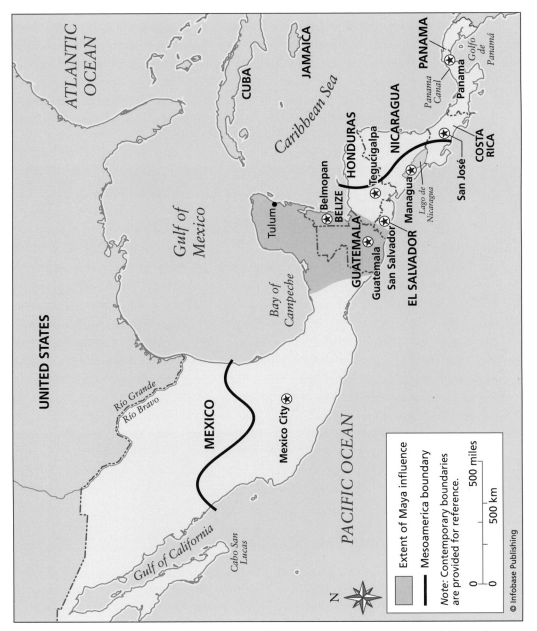

In the modern world the Maya influence would have stretched across Mexico's Yucatán Peninsula, Guatemala, Belize, and parts of El Salvador and Honduras.

where farming the steep slopes is terribly difficult and largely unprofitable.

Although the Guatemalan government made some attempts between 1945 and 1954 to treat the Maya with more dignity, the U.S. government prevented land grants and social improvements. During this time, the American United Fruit Company (AUFC) owned more land in Guatemala than any other company. Fearing profits would be hurt by Maya farm ownership, the AUFC requested that the U.S. State Department intervene.

With support from the United States, the Guatemalan government was overthrown in a violent coup (an illegal seizure of power) in 1954.

Searching from Space

Archaeologists have teamed up with NASA scientists to search for ancient Maya cities. Orbiting surveillance satellites take pictures of the Maya area. The photos reveal the outlines of ancient buildings under the dense jungle growth. Most Maya builders used limestone and lime plaster. Chemicals from the lime seep into the ground and act like a weed killer on many of the naturally growing plants in the area. The chemicals also change the color of some plants. Normally, jungle growth would hide most of the Maya buildings and platforms. But because of the chemicals released into the soil, the plants reveal outlines of structures that can be seen from space.

These three images show the ruins of a Maya city in the Petén region of Guatemala. The top one was taken from a helicopter and shows how the dense trees make the ruins just about invisible. The middle image was made by NASA, using data from satellites. The bottom image shows structures that were found using the NASA images.

The new military government was so corrupt that thousands of Maya chose to flee their homeland in fear for their lives. Those who remained and spoke out against the corruption were imprisoned or executed.

The series of military regimes unleashed attacks against the Maya unlike anything since the Spanish conquest. More than 150,000 people were killed, and another 40,000 went missing. In the 1980s, thousands of Maya sought refuge in camps in Mexico and thousands more fled to the United States.

The suffering of the Maya in Guatemala was not relieved until December of 1995, when a new government took power in Guatemala. Although things are far from ideal for the Maya today in Guatemala, they have come far from the terror of the past. They have the protection of the law to celebrate their cultural identity and resettle on ancestral lands. Schools teach Mayan languages. And the Maya finally have a voice in the government—their own voice, spoken by their own people. Not all of the discrimination has been extinguished, but the Maya are increasing in numbers and are determined not to be silenced again.

THE MAYA TODAY

One of the most isolated and traditional groups of Maya live in the jungles of the lowlands in the Mexican state of Chiapas, near the southern border with Guatemala. They are the Lacandon, and they speak one of the 30 Mayan languages used today. The Lacandon are closely tied to the ways of their ancestors. They continue to worship the same gods, practice the same customs, and make stone tools from flint quarried in the rainforest.

They live in houses with thatched roofs. The women weave colorful fabrics in designs that show where they live, who their ancestors were, and which gods—rain, fertility, health—they wish to please. The men still tend corn fields and join together to build homes as their families grow. There are holy men who "keep the days" of the 260-day sacred Maya calendar, using corn kernels to count days and their ancestral knowledge to foretell the future.

One of the last Maya chiefs of the Lacandon, Chan K'in, continued to make clay pots as offerings to the gods until he died in 1996. These are now sold by his son to tourists in Palenque. But even the Lacandon are finding it difficult to hold out against outside influences. One by one, their children are leaving to join the modern world.

Modern Maya greet the north during a celebration of the Maya new year in Guatemala. The Maya make up about half of Guatemala's population.

If the ways of the old ones are no longer to be practiced in the modern world, there will still be reminders of the great civilization of the Maya in the volcanic highlands and jungle lowlands of Central America. The Maya left their mark on the landscape in majestic stone structures that are being mapped from outer space. Using advanced imaging technology, scientists are pinpointing ruins that have been hidden for 2,000 years or more.

When archaeologists on the ground uncover these new finds, they describe these wondrous cities with the same reverence as John Stephens, the 19th century explorer who first enchanted the modern world with his descriptions of Copán in *Incidents of Travel in Central America*. When Stephens's Maya guide whacked away a thousand years of jungle growth with vigorous strokes of a machete and revealed 14 ancient monuments, Stephens wrote, "one displaced from its pedestal by enormous roots; another locked in close embrace of branches and trees, and almost lifted out of the earth; another hurled to the ground, and bound down by huge vines and creepers; and one standing, with its altar before it, in a grove of trees which grew around it, seemingly to shade and shroud it as a sacred thing; in solemn stillness of the woods, it seemed a divinity mourning over fallen people."

TIME LINE

6000–2000 B.C.E.	During the Archaic Era, there is a gradual transition from hunter-gatherers to settled village life.
3114 B.C.E.	August 11 is the first day of the Long Count calendar.
1200 B.C.E.–250 C.E.	The Preclassic Era
1200–1000 B.C.E.	During the Early Preclassic Period, the culture that will soon be identified as Maya rises alongside earlier Mesoamerican cultures such as the Olmec.
1000–400 B.C.E.	During the Middle Preclassic Period, Maya chiefdoms along the Pacific Coast and in the highlands appear and flourish. The lowlands are colonized. Monument building begins.
600 B.C.E.	The Maya at Kaminaljuyú dig irrigation canals.
400 B.C.E.– 250 C.E.	Curing the Late Preclassic Period, urban centers appear. The highland Maya decline while the lowland Maya flourish. Dynastic rulers are named and their dates of rule recorded in Long Count form on monuments, temples, and tombs.
250–900	The Classic Era
250–600	The Early Classic Period is the golden age of many capital cities, including Tikal, Calakmul, Copán, Caracol, Palenque, Yaxchilán, and Piedras Negras. Long-distance trade thrives.
600–800	During the Late Classic Period, warfare increases. Increasingly, trade comes under the control of elite leaders at large centers. Some of the greatest building achievements and largest populations are in cities of the southern lowlands. The "superpowers" Tikal and Calakmul battle over the control of the Maya world, but neither achieves total or lasting control.
800–900	During the Terminal Classic Period, the cities in the central and southern lowlands decline. New cities rise in Yucatán and the highlands. Tikal, Calakmul, Copán, and most of the southern lowland sites are abandoned. People move north and to sites along lakes, rivers, and coastal areas.
900–1524	During the Postclassic Era, the capitals in the northern Yucatán and along the coasts prosper. Local trade and long-distance trade with Central Mexico and Central America increases. Trade routes shift from overland routes through the (now largely uninhabited) southern lowlands to coastal and some river routes.
1502	Christopher Columbus first makes contact with seagoing Maya traders.

1511	The Maya first encounter Europeans on their mainland.
1517	Spaniard Francisco Hernández de Córdoba leads the first extensive European exploration of the Maya area.
1519	The first major attack is launched against the Maya by Hernán Cortés, near present-day Cozumel.
1521	Plague kills one third of highland population.
1524–1697	The Spanish conquer and colonize the Maya area.
1697	In March, the Spanish military puts down the last Maya uprising in the Yucatán and declares the conquest of the Maya complete.
1821	Mexico wins independence from Spain.
1847–1901	In the War of the Castes, Maya people in the Yucatán battle for independence from Mexico.
1910	The Maya in Mexico obtain equal rights.
1995	A new government in Guatemala ends a long period of repression against the Maya.
2012	December 21 is the last day of the current cycle of the Long Count calendar.

GLOSSARY

adobe mud that is hardened into a building material by drying it in the sun

alliance a friendship or bond between groups of people or nations

altar an elevated structure, such as a mound or platform, where religious ceremonies are performed or sacrifices are made to the gods or ancestors

ancestor a person from whom one is descended

archaeologist a scientist who studies ancient people by studying the items they left behind

architecture the way buildings are designed and built; a person who designs buildings is an *architect*

artisan a skilled worker who makes things by hand

barter to trade goods or services for items considered by both parties to be of equal value

basalt black rock formed from hardened lava

bas-relief sculpture where figures project out from the background

bloodletting spilling one's own blood as part of a ritual

cacao the plant from which chocolate is made

causeway a raised road

cenote a natural well or sinkhole in limestone, with a pool at the bottom

cinnabar a mineral that can be used to make brilliant red dyes

city-state a city that functions as a separate kingdom or nation

clan a group of close-knit families

codex an early form of a book with pages (replacing books written on scrolls); the plural is *codices*

colonize migrate to an area and settle down

colonnade a series of evenly spaced columns supporting a roof

commerce the exchange of goods on a large scale, between countries or regions within a country

commodities articles for trade or commerce

conquistador the Spanish word for "conqueror"

decapitate to cut off the head

deity a god or goddess

descendants all a person's offspring

divination the practice of predicting the future

dynasty a sequence of rulers from the same family

elite persons of the highest class

fertile able to easily grow (for plants) or have offspring (for animals and people)

glyph a character or symbol used in writing

hearth fireplace

heir a person who inherits belongings, title, rank, or position from a deceased person

hierarchy a system where people are ranked one above the other

hieroglyph a stylized picture of an object representing a word, syllable, or sound

k'atun the Maya cycle of 7,200 days

kin Mayan word for "day"

linguist a person who studies languages

lintel a horizontal support over a window or door

maize corn

Mesoamerica meaning "middle America," the area extending from what is today central Mexico to Honduras and Nicaragua

mural wall painting

myth a traditional story, often with a magical element

nobles people belonging to a special (and elite) social or political class

obsidian volcanic glass

omen a sign or event that foretells the future

pagan from a primitive religion; a person who is not a Christian

polity an organized society with a system of government

polytheism worshipping more than one god

pre-Columbian before the arrival of Christopher Columbus in the Americas in 1492

quarry to dig out

reign the length of time a particular ruler is in power

ritual a ceremony carried out according to religious laws and customs

scepter a ceremonial staff that is held in the hand as a symbol of power and authority

scribe a person who copies out documents

shaman a person who has access to and influence over good and evil spirits

stela a stone pillar with an inscription on it; the plural is *stelae*

successor a person who follows another in an office or position

terrace an elevated garden plot

terracing building a number of flat platforms, usually into the side of a hill: *terrace farming* is farming the land on these flat platforms

thatch a roof covering made of palm fronds, straw, or leaves

trance a semi-conscious state

tribute something of value paid by one state to another as proof of loyalty or obedience, or to secure peace or protection

BIBLIOGRAPHY

Brainerd, George W., *The Maya Civilization.* Los Angles: Southwest Museum, 1954.

Coe, Michael D., *The Maya.* New York: Thames and Hudson, 1999.

Cortés, Fernando, *His Five Letters of Relation to the Emperor Charles V.* Francis Augustus MacNutt, translator. Glorieta, New Mexico: Rio Grande Press, Inc. 1977.

Cortés, Hernán, *Letters from Mexico.* Anthony Pagden, translator and editor. New Haven, Conn.: Yale University Press, 1986.

Craine, Eugene R. and Reginald C. Reindorp, translators, *The Codex Perez and the Book of Chilam Balam of Mani.* Norman, Okla.: University of Oklahoma Press, 1979.

Culbert, T. Patrick, *Smithsonian Exploring the Ancient World: Maya Civilization.* Washington, D.C.: Smithsonian Books, 1993.

Danziger, Eve, *Relatively Speaking: Language, Thought, and Kinship among the Mopan Maya.* New York: Oxford University Press, 2001.

Demarest, Arthur, *Ancient Maya: The Rise and Fall of a Rainforest Civilization.* Cambridge, UK: Cambridge University Press, 2004.

Diamond, Jared, *Collapse: How Societies Choose to Fail or Succeed.* New York: Viking, 2005.

"The Enduring Maya. Guatemala and Mexico: The Maya Today." Exploring the World. Available online. URL: http://www.culturefocus.com/guatemala_maya.htm. Accessed October 31, 2008.

Finley, Michael, "Astronomy in the Codices." The Real Maya Prophecies: Astronomy in the Inscriptions and Codices. Available online. URL: http://members.shaw.ca/mjfinley/codex.html. Accessed October 17, 2008.

Foster, Lynn V., *Handbook to Life in the Ancient Maya World.* New York: Facts On File, 2002.

"The Fourth Voyage of Christopher Columbus (1502)." *Athena Review,* vol. 2, no. 1. Available online. URL: http://www.athenapub.com/coluvoy4.htm. Accessed October 31, 2008.

Fuentes, Patricia de, editor and translator, *The Conquistadors: First-person Accounts of the Conquest of Mexico.* Norman, Okla.: University of Oklahoma Press, 1963.

Graber, Karen Hursh, "Los Tamales: 500 Years at the Heart of the Fiesta." Mexico Connect. Available online. URL: http://www.mexconnect.com/mex_/recipes/puebla/kgtamales.html. Accessed October 15, 2008.

"Guatemala History." Encyclopedia of the Nations. Available online, URL: http://www.nationsencyclopedia.com/Americas/Guatemala-HISTORY.html. Accessed November 6, 2008.

Harrup, Anthony, "History of Mexico." Mexperience. Available online. URL: http://www.mexperience.com/history/. Accessed November 3, 2008.

Hassig, Ross, *Mexico and the Spanish Conquest.* New York: Longman, 1994.

Henderson, John S., *The World of the Ancient Maya.* Ithaca, N.Y.: Cornell University Press, 1997.

Hofling, Charles Andres, *Itzá Maya Texts.* Salt Lake City: University of Utah Press, 1991.

Honan, William H., "Did Maya Doom Themselves By Felling Trees?" The *New York Times,* April 11, 1995. Available online. URL: http://query.nytimes.com/gst/fullpage.html?res=990CE5DF1339F932A25757C0A963958260. Accessed September 31, 2008.

James, Peter and Nick Thorpe, *Ancient Inventions.* New York: Ballentine Books, 1994.

Johns, Chris, editor, *The Mysteries of the Maya.* Washington, D.C.: National Geographic Society, 2008.

Jones, Grant D., *Maya Resistance to Spanish Rule: Time and History on a Colonial Frontier.* Albuquerque, N.Mex: University of New Mexico Press, 1989.

Kramer, Karen L., *Maya Children: Helpers at the Farm.* Cambridge, Mass.: Harvard University Press, 2005.

Landa, Diego de, *Yucatan Before and After the Conquest.* William Gates, translator. New York: Dover, 1978.

Latham, William, "Guatemala: Heart of the Mayan World." Adventure Learning Foundation. Available online. URL: http://www.questconnect.org/guat_heart_mayan_world.htm. Accessed September 28, 2008.

Laughton, Timothy, *The Maya: Life, Myth, and Art.* New York: Stewart, Tabori & Chang, 1998.

"Lost King of the Maya." Nova Online. Available online. URL: http://www.pbs.org/wgbh/nova/maya/copa_transcript.html#11. Accessed October 13, 2008.

Martin, Simon and Nikolai Grube, *Chronicle of the Maya Kings and Queens: Deciphering the Dynasties of the Ancient Maya.* London: Thames and Hudson, 2000.

McKillop, Heather, *The Ancient Maya: New Perspectives.* New York: W. W. Norton & Company, 2006.

Miller, Mary Ellen, *The Art of Mesoamerica from Olmec to Aztec.* London: Thames and Hudson, 1990.

Miller, Mary Ellen, *Maya Art and Architecture.* London: Thames and Hudson, 1999.

Phillips, Charles, *The Illustrated Encyclopedia of Aztec & Maya: The History, Legend, Myth and Culture of the Ancient Native Peoples of Mexico and Central America.* London: Anness Publishing Ltd., 2004.

Porter III, Frank W., *Indians of North America: The Maya.* New York: Chelsea House Publishers, 1991.

Proskouriakoff, Tatiana, *An Album of Maya Architecture,* Norman, Okla.: University of Oklahoma Press, 1963.

——, *Maya History.* Austin, Texas: University of Texas Press, 1993.

Restall, Matthew, *The Maya World: Yucatec Culture and Society, 1550-1850.* Stanford, Calif.: Stanford University Press, 1997.

Roys, Ralph L., translator, *The Book of Chilam Balam of Chumayel.* Washington, D.C.: Carnegie Institution, 1933.

——, *Ritual of the Bacabs: a Book of Mayan Incantations.* Norman, Okla.: University of Oklahoma Press, 1965.

Ruddell, Nancy, *Mystery of the Maya.* Hull, Quebec: Canadian Museum of Civilization, 1995.

Sabloff, Jeremy A., *The New Archaeology and the Ancient Maya.* New York: Scientific American Library, 1990.

Sawyer-Lauçanno, Christopher, *The Destruction of the Jaguar: Poems form the Books of Chilam Balam.* San Francisco: City Lights Books, 1987.

Schele, Linda, and David Freidel, *A Forest of Kings: The Untold Story of the Ancient Maya.* New York: Quill William Morrow, 1990.

Schele, Linda, and Peter Mathews, *The Code of Kings: The Language of Seven Sacred Maya Temples and Tombs.* New York: Scribner, 1998.

Schele, Linda, and Mary Ellen Miller, *The Blood of Kings: Dynasty and Ritual in Maya Art.* New York: George Braziller, Inc., 1986.

Sharer, Robert J., *The Ancient Maya.* Stanford, Calif.: Stanford University Press, 2006.

——, *Daily Life in Maya Civilization.* Westport, Conn.: Greenwood Press, 1996.

Smith, Herman, "Dig It." Articles on Archaeology and the Maya on Ambergris Caye, Belize. Available online. URL: http://ambergriscaye.com/museum/digit.html. Accessed October 31, 2008.

Stephens, John Lloyd, *Incidents of Travel.* "Lost King of the Maya." Available online. URL: http://www.pbs.org/wgbh/nova/maya/travel.html. Accessed September 23, 2008.

Stierlin, Henri, *Living Architecture: Mayan.* New York: Grosset & Dunlap, 1964.

Stuart, Gene S. and George E. Stuart, *Lost Kingdoms of the Maya.* Washington D.C.: National Geographic Society, 1993.

Tedlock, Dennis, translator, *Popol Vuh: The Mayan Book of the Dawn of Life.* New York: Simon & Schuster, 1996.

Teresi, Dick, *Lost Discoveries: The Ancient Roots of Modern Science—from the Babylonians to the Maya.* New York: Simon & Schuster, 2002.

Trout, Lawana Hooper, *The Maya.* New York: Chelsea House, 1991.

"Unmasking the Maya: The Story of Sna Jtz'ibajom." Smithsonian Institution, National Museum of Natural History. Available online. URL: http://anthropology.si.edu/maya/mayaprint.html. Accessed November 1, 2008.

Willard, Theodore A., *The Lost Empires of the Itzaes and Mayas: An American Civilization, contemporary with Christ, which rivaled the Culture of Egypt.* Glendale, Calif.: Arthur H. Clark Company, 1933.

FURTHER RESOURCES

BOOKS

Coulter, Laurie, *Ballplayers and Bone Setters: 100 Ancient Aztec and Maya Jobs You Might Have Adored or Abhorred* (Toronto, Canada: Annick Press, 2008)

> The ancient Aztecs, Maya, and other Mesoamericans believed that the gods created a world where everyone had a role to play. Some people were born to rule, others to serve. The lucky ones might have been a high priest or a queen. Others could have ended up as a farmer, a slave, or sacrificial victim. Find out in this book what it was like to be a tax collector, a porter, a pyramid builder, a beekeeper, and a royal cook.

Johns, Chris, editor, *Mysteries of the Maya* (Washington D.C.: National Geographic Society, 2008)

> Lively science writers present the rise, glory, and collapse of the Maya civilization, coupled with National Geographic's breathtaking photography. Four sections cover the Preclassic Era to today's Maya.

Laughton, Timothy, *The Maya: Life, Myth, and Art* (New York: Stewart, Tabori & Chang, 1998)

> In this beautifully illustrated book, Laughton shows how the daily life of the ancient Maya was filled with ritual. The supernatural world is the foundation of Maya art and architecture—even their games. Laughton provides interpretations of Maya images of sacrifice, ritual, and myth, as well as explanations of how the Maya used their calendars to predict the future.

Perl, Lila, *The Ancient Maya* (New York: Franklin Watts, 2005)

> Perl explores the ancient Maya culture through gods and priests, farmers and kings, scribes and artists, warriors and traders. Little is known about the individuals who practiced these roles. But their place in the social fabric can be deduced from present-day archaeological discoveries and from accounts written by the Spaniards who occupied the Maya area following the Postclassic Era. Perl draws on these resources to recreate life in ancient Maya times.

Phillips, Charles, *The Illustrated Encyclopedia of Aztec & Maya: The History, Legend, Myth and Culture of the Ancient Native Peoples of Mexico and Central America* (London: Anness Publishing Ltd., 2004)

> This lavishly illustrated volume introduces the myths of ancient Mesoamerica. Grouped according to subject—creation and the first peoples, earth and sky, harvest, after death—the reader gains insight into how the Maya viewed their world.

Sharer, Robert J., *Daily Life in Maya Civilization* (Westport, Conn.: Greenwood Press, 1996)

> Robert J. Sharer is the Shoemaker Professor of Anthropology at the University of Pennsylvania and Curator of the American Section at the university's Museum of Archaeology and Anthropology. His 40 years of experience studying the Maya are apparent in this vibrant reconstruction of Maya society. Through his field work at archaeological sites in the Maya region, Sharer not only corrects popular misconceptions, but also brings evidence for new interpretations of what life was like for the ancient Maya. At the close of each chapter, Sharer suggests relevant publications that are "current, accessible, and significant"—just as this book most certainly is.

Stuart, Gene S. and George E. Stuart, *Lost King-doms of the Maya* (Washington D.C.: National Geographic Society, 1993)

> Rich storytelling by the Stuarts, who have spent decades working in the Maya area, brings the discovery and conquest of the Maya to life. And of course, National Geographic photography in all its glory takes the reader there as well. The Stuarts look into the lives of the ancient Maya—their cosmic view, their cities, their art and architecture, their religion and ritual. This book closes by introducing the reader to today's Maya and their rich culture, which is a blend of old and new.

Tucker, Mary, *Mayans and Aztecs: Exploring Ancient Civilizations* (Carthage, Ill.: Teaching & Learning Company, 2002)

> Ancient history will come to life, for the reader can design a battle uniform based on Maya thinking, and also learn about the diet, work, entertainment, worship, and warfare of these ancient cultures.

DVDS

Cracking the Maya Code (Nova, PBS, 2008)

> This episode of the PBS series *Nova* presents the story of how Maya hieroglyphics were decoded, told by the experts at the center of one of archaeology's great detective stories. It highlights the breakthroughs that opened the door to deciphering the exotic script and finally cracked the code, giving historians dramatic new insights into ancient Maya civilization

Dawn of the Maya (National Geographic, 2004)

> This National Geographic special looks at the Maya in the Preclassic Era. It focuses on recent archaeological discoveries that have uncovered new information about the early years of the ancient Maya. This information reveals a dynamic, sophisticated culture. The Preclassic Maya created massive pyramids, elaborate art, early writing styles, and more.

WEB SITES

Authentic Maya
www.authenticmaya.com/authentic_maya.htm

> More than 110 Guatemalan archaeological sites from the Maya Preclassic and Classic Era are covered in this Web site. The well-organized links lead to everything from medicine to warfare. Texts of classic Maya mythology, such as *Popol Vuh*, can also be accessed here.

Dig It
http://ambergriscaye.com/museum/digit.html

> Archaeologist Dr. Herman Smith presents mini-lectures on the Maya from his work at the Maya site Ambergris Caye in Belize. The humorous lectures also explore what it is like to be an archaeologist and what the job entails, including some of the hazards, such as snakes!

FAMSI: The Foundation for the Advancement of Mesoamerican Studies, Inc.
www.famsi.org

> This site covers all the cultures of Mesoamerica. It includes details on major archaeological sites from the Preclassic Era to the Postclassic Era, including history, maps, a "who's who" in the ancient Maya world, and a large number of photos. The section on Mayan hieroglyphic writing shows the four surviving codices, along with annotations. Archaeologists write about recent archaeological research funded by FAMSI. Maya scholars use this site extensively. A Spanish translation is also available.

Lost King of the Maya
www.pbs.org/wgbh/nova/maya/

> This site, linked with the PBS series *Nova*, tours Copán with guide David Stuart. When he was a boy, Stuart copied glyphs with his crayons while his father worked as an archaeologist in the Maya area. In his teens, he helped crack the code of Maya hieroglyphs. Interactive pages enable you to read carved stelae by clicking on the glyphs and to hear the Mayan words spoken. Included are teacher's guides, interviews, interactive activities, and more.

Maya Calendar Tools

www.pauahtun.org/Calendar/tools.html

Find any date in the Long with the Maya calendar conversion tools provided. This site also shows Mayan glyphs for calendar related words such as months and numbers.

Maya History Timeline

www.oneworldjourneys.com/jaguar/mayan_timeline.html

This annotated timeline spotlights Maya cultural highlights. Included are short sketches of neighboring civilizations that share jaguar gods.

Maya Rise and Fall

http://ngm.nationalgeographic.com/2007/08/maya-rise-fall/

This site is from National Geographic, and details the rise, flowering, and eventual collapse of Maya civilization. The site includes articles and many photos from archaeological sites. An excellent interactive map shows you what has been found at each archaeological dig. There are also Q&A features with the photographer and journalist who wrote the articles in the site, and a large photo gallery.

Museo Popol Vuh

http://maya-archaeology.org/museums/popolvuh/kamina.html

This site contains hundreds of images of pre-Columbian Maya art, stone and ceramic sculpture, and is designed to showcase the talents of Maya artists and scribes. For a deeper understanding of the context of the artwork, follow the links to Maya archaeological sites and private museums.

The Real Maya Prophecies: Astronomy in the Inscriptions and Codices

http://members.shaw.ca/mjfinley/mainmaya.html

The Maya developed one the most sophisticated calendar systems of any ancient culture. At this site, primary sources reveal events Maya astronomers calculated with incredible accuracy, such as lunar eclipses and solar years. Glyphs, bas-reliefs, and codices are illustrated and decoded to show how Maya priests used calendars to foretell the future. The site also exposes sloppy science when common Maya myths are debunked.

The Topic: Maya

www.42explore2.com/maya.htm

Become a Maya explorer by following the links. This site offers a section on Maya children, with a kid-friendly blog that introduces dozens of Maya cities. It also has links to fun activities, such as coloring pages and foods Maya children eat today.

PICTURE CREDITS

INDEX

Note: **Boldface** page numbers indicate major discussions of topics; *italic* page numbers indicate illustrations; page numbers followed by *c* indicate chronology entries; page numbers followed by *g* indicate glossary entries; page numbers followed by *m* indicate maps.

ABOUT THE AUTHOR

JILL RUBALCABA began her working life teaching mathematics in college and high school in Boston, all the while continuing her education in math, writing, and business. Later she worked as an engineer on the Patriot Missile in Massachusetts and in White Sands, New Mexico. She is the author of *A Place in the Sun, The Wadjet Eye, The Early Human World, The Ancient Egyptian World*, and *National Geographic Investigates Ancient Egypt.* Jill lives on the Wesleyan campus in Middletown, Connecticut, with her husband, Daniel, and her cats, Me and Metoo.

Historical consultant **ANGELA H. KELLER, PH.D.** is an archaeologist with more than 15 years of experience working in Mesoamerica, the United States, and Europe. She has excavated everything from Paleolithic camp sites to ancient Maya burial crypts and has never been attacked by mummies, angry locals, or aliens. She teaches anthropology at the University of California, Riverside. Angela did her doctoral research in Belize, where she investigated the roads of the Classic Maya center of Xunantunich. Currently, she is affiliated with the Chan Archaeological Project in Belize.